Writing the American Past

In memory of Michael J. Lea, a true original

Writing the American Past

US History to 1877

Mark M. Smith

WILEY-BLACKWELL

A John Wiley & Sons, Ltd., Publication

This edition first published 2009

Blackwell Publishing was acquired by John Wiley & Sons in February 2007. Blackwell's publishing program has been merged with Wiley's global Scientific, Technical, and Medical business to form Wiley-Blackwell.

Registered Office
John Wiley & Sons Ltd, The Atrium, Southern Gate, Chichester, West Sussex, PO19 8SQ, United Kingdom

Editorial Offices
350 Main Street, Malden, MA 02148-5020, USA
9600 Garsington Road, Oxford, OX4 2DQ, UK
The Atrium, Southern Gate, Chichester, West Sussex, PO19 8SQ, UK

For details of our global editorial offices, for customer services, and for information about how to apply for permission to reuse the copyright material in this book please see our website at www.wiley.com/wiley-blackwell.

Library of Congress Cataloging-in-Publication Data

Writing the American past : US history to 1877 / [edited by] Mark M. Smith.
p. cm.
Includes bibliographical references and index.
ISBN 978-1-4051-6359-0 (pbk. : alk. paper) 1. United States–History–Colonial period, ca. 1600–1775–Sources. 2. United States–History–Revolution, 1775–1783–Sources. 3. United States–History–1783–1865–Sources. 4. United States–History–1865–1898–Sources. 5. United States–History–Study and teaching. I. Smith, Mark M. (Mark Michael), 1968–
E187.W75 2009
973–dc22

2008042457

A catalogue record for this book is available from the British Library.

Set in 11/12.5pt Dante
by SPi Publisher Services, Pondicherry, India
Printed in Singapore by Fabulous Printers Pte Ltd

01 2009

Contents

Timeline

1492	Courtesy of the Spanish Crown, Christopher Columbus makes the first of four voyages to the New World.
1497	John Cabot of England explores the coast of Canada and claims it for Henry VII.
1499	Italian navigator, Amerigo Vespucci, sights the coast of South America (again, for the Spanish).
1513	Ponce de León of Spain lands in Florida.
1517	Martin Luther launches the Protestant Reformation.
1524	French-sponsored Giovanni da Verrazano explores the Carolinas, the Hudson River, and Nova Scotia.
1565	First permanent European colony in North America founded at St. Augustine (Florida) by the Spanish.
1588	England defeats Spain militarily in Europe leading to the decline of Spanish influence in the New World and the beginning of English imperial interests.
1606	The London Company sponsors an expedition to Virginia.
1607	Jamestown founded in Virginia.
1609	Tobacco first planted and harvested in Virginia by colonists.
1613	Dutch establish trading post on Manhattan Island.
1616	Tobacco becomes an export staple for Virginia.
1616	Smallpox epidemic kills many Native Americans in New England.
1619	First legislative assembly in America convenes in Virginia.
1619	Twenty Africans brought by the Dutch to Jamestown for sale as indentured servants.
1620	*Mayflower* lands in Massachusetts.
1624	Virginia declared a Royal colony.

1630	John Winthrop leads a Puritan migration of 900 colonists to Massachusetts Bay.
1636	Roger Williams founds Providence and Rhode Island.
1638	Anne Hutchinson banished from Massachusetts for nonconformist religious views.
1640–59	English Civil War between the Royalists of King Charles I and the Parliamentary army; latter prevails and England becomes a Commonwealth and Protectorate ruled by Oliver Cromwell.
1652	Rhode Island outlaws slavery.
1660	English monarchy restored under King Charles II.
1660	English Crown approves a Navigation Act requiring the exclusive use of English ships for trade in English colonies.
1664	Maryland passes a law making lifelong servitude for black slaves mandatory.
1675–6	King Philip's War in New England between colonists and Native Americans.
1692	Salem witchcraft trials.
1720	Population of American colonists: 475,000.
1725	Number of black slaves in the American colonies: 75,000.
1732–57	Benjamin Franklin publishes *Poor Richard's Almanac.*
1739	England declares war on Spain.
1743	American Philosophical Society founded in Philadelphia.
1747	The New York Bar Association is founded in New York City.
1754	French and Indian War breaks out.
1760	Colonial population reaches 1,500,000; George III ascends the throne.
1763	French and Indian War ends with the Treaty of Paris.
1763	Pontiac's Rebellion.
1763	The Proclamation of 1763 prohibits English settlement west of the Appalachian Mountains.
1764	Sugar Act passed by Parliament.
1765	Stamp Act passed by Parliament.
1765	Patrick Henry presents Virginia Resolutions.
1765	Sons of Liberty form in opposition to the Stamp Act.
1765	Stamp Act Congress petitions the King and Parliament to repeal the Stamp Act.
1766	English Parliament repeals the Stamp Act but passes the Declaratory Act stating that the British government has authority to legislate law in the American colonies.
1767	Parliament passes the Townshend Revenue Acts.
1768	Samuel Adams of Massachusetts opposes taxation without representation and calls for the colonists to unite against the British government.
1769	Philadelphia merchants join the emerging boycott of British trade goods.
	Boycott spreads to New Jersey, Rhode Island, and North Carolina.
1770	Population of the American colonies: 2,210,000.
	Boston Massacre occurs.
1772	Colonies establish committees of correspondence to coordinate protest.
1773	Boston Tea Party.
1774	Parliament passes the first of a series of Coercive Acts in response to resistance in Massachusetts. Boston Port Bill closes commercial shipping in Boston harbor. First Continental Congress meets in Philadelphia.

1775	Massachusetts Governor Gage enforces the Coercive Acts and orders British soldiers to Concord to destroy the colonists' weapons depot. Battles at Lexington and Concord ensue.
April 1775	Provincial Congress in Massachusetts orders 13,600 American soldiers mobilized. Colonists begin a year-long siege of British-held Boston.
June 1775	Second Continental Congress appoints George Washington commander-in-chief of the Continental Army. In July, Congress issues a Declaration on the Causes and Necessity of Taking Up Arms against the British.
January 1776	Thomas Paine publishes *Common Sense*.
July 1776	Congress formally endorses Thomas Jefferson's draft of the Declaration of Independence. Copies sent to colonies.
1783	Peace of Paris.
1787	Constitutional Congress meets and submits the Constitution to the states for ratification.
1788	States ratify Constitution.
1789	George Washington elected President.
1790	Samuel Slater's cotton mill established in Rhode Island.
1793	Practical gin for short-staple cotton invented and cotton cultivation spreads westward.
1801	Raw cotton output reaches about 100,000 bales per year.
1803	Louisiana Purchase more than doubles the size of the United States.
1808	Further importation of slaves banned by Congress.
1812	War with Britain.
1815	Peace of Ghent.
1819	Panic of 1819.
1820	5.5 percent of southerners live in an urban area; figure for New England is 10.5 percent.
1820	Missouri Compromise.
1822	Cotton mills opened in Lowell, Massachusetts.
1822	A slave insurrection planned by Denmark Vesey in Charleston, South Carolina, is uncovered.
1828	Andrew Jackson elected president.
	John C. Calhoun's South Carolina Exposition and Protest outlines the right of a state to nullify an act of Congress deemed unconstitutional by the state.
1831	William Lloyd Garrison begins publication of *The Liberator* calling for immediate emancipation of southern slaves.
1831	Nat Turner's Rebellion in Southampton County, Virginia.
1832	South Carolina issues Ordinance of Nullification.
1833	Chicago founded.
1835	Raw cotton output reaches about 1 million bales a year.
1837	Panic of 1837 inaugurates prolonged depression.
1840	Percentage of the South's population living in an urban environment is 7.7; for New England, 19.4 percent; for the Mid-Atlantic states, 18.1 percent.
1846	United States declares war on Mexico.
	Wilmot Proviso attempts to ban slavery from any territory acquired as a result of the war with Mexico.
1850	The Compromise of 1850 attempts to resolve the growing crisis between North and South over the westward expansion of slavery.

1852	Harriet Beecher Stowe publishes *Uncle Tom's Cabin.*
1854	The Kansas-Nebraska Act repeals the Missouri Compromise.
1856	Preston S. Brooks of South Carolina canes Senator Charles Sumner of Massachusetts on the floor of the United States Senate.
1857	Dred Scott decision.
	Chief Justice Robert B. Taney rules that African Americans, even free ones, are not citizens.
1859	John Brown's raid.
1860	South has 3.84 million slaves. 11.5 percent of the South's population lives in towns or cities. In New England, the figure is 36.6 percent; in the Mid-Atlantic states, 35.4 percent.
1860	Abraham Lincoln elected President.
1860–1	Southern states secede from the Union.
1861	Civil War breaks out.
September 1861	Lincoln revokes General John C. Frémont's unauthorized military proclamation of emancipation in Missouri.
April 1862	Union navy takes New Orleans.
September 1862	Battle at Antietam: Confederates under General Robert E. Lee are stopped; Lee withdraws to Virginia. Lincoln issues preliminary Emancipation Proclamation freeing slaves.
January 1863	Lincoln issues the final Emancipation Proclamation freeing all slaves in territories held by Confederates. The war to preserve the Union is now one to end slavery.
May 1863	Union Army is defeated by Lee's smaller force at the Battle of Chancellorsville, Virginia.
June 1863	Lee launches his second invasion of the North, which will result in defeat at Gettysburg.
July 1863	Confederates lose Vicksburg. Confederacy is now bisected.
November 1863	Lincoln delivers Gettysburg Address.
September 1864	Sherman captures Atlanta and in November marches to Savannah.
January 1865	US Congress approves the Thirteenth Amendment abolishing slavery.
April 1865	Lee surrenders to General Ulysses S. Grant at Appomattox Court House, Virginia. Lincoln assassinated; Vice President Andrew Johnson assumes the presidency.
May 1865	Remaining Confederate forces surrender. Over 620,000 Americans die in the war.
1865	Southern states enact "Black codes" to limit the movement of freedpeople.
1866	Congress proposes Fourteenth Amendment providing citizenship to ex-slaves; emergence of Ku Klux Klan.
1867	Congressional Reconstruction underway.
1868	Fourteenth Amendment ratified.
1870	Fifteenth Amendment ratified.
1873	Economic Panic.
1877	Reconstruction ends.

Acknowledgments

Archivists and scholars from around the United States have been extraordinarily generous and helpful in helping me assemble this volume. My sincere thanks to the staff at the various libraries and archives for their attention to detail and, on occasions, their impeccable detective work. Specifically, my thanks to Allen Stokes, Trenton Hizer, and Mary Linnemann in this regard. I am also indebted to Aaron Marrs and Cheryl Wells for providing me with references to some key documents. Thanks also to Bob Ellis for his careful proof-reading. My graduate student, David Prior, was simply indispensable when it came to helping me identify sources and I still marvel at his efficiency, good cheer, and tenacity. He has my sincere thanks. At Wiley-Blackwell, Deidre Ilkson was marvelously supportive. Tom Bates and Simon Eckley did wonders on the technical side and I'm in their debt. As for Peter Coveney – well, I'll say, simply, that any author would be hard pressed to find a better editor. I am most grateful for their kindness and support.

Editor's Introduction:
History, Handed Down

The past is not always easily accessed. Much of it does not come to us neatly typed, in easily deciphered documents. Often, it survives in handwritten, sometimes scribbled form, the writing sometimes cramped and difficult to read, perhaps composed in poor light, at desks, on trains, or in open fields. More than that, time damages paper, lightens ink, and smudges pencil; insects nibble, pages tear, fingers erase, holes and tears gobble parts of words so that reading documents from the past is sometimes a difficult affair. And when these documents are available only in photocopied form, survive only on scratchy microfilm, challenges mount. Stingy with their information, handwritten documents often yield their secrets slowly, demand that we read with care and patience, decipher intelligently, and remember the preeminent importance of historical context. *Writing the American Past* helps students master these skills.

This book reproduces images of dozens of primary sources and handwritten documents and, in effect, brings them from the archives to the classroom. It introduces students to the exciting, challenging, and satisfying art of working with untranscribed historical documents from the 1690s to the 1860s. The documents speak to some of the most important themes in US history from a number of perspectives. Women and slaves, businessmen and politicians, southerners, northerners, and Midwesterners talk about religion, war, liberty, business, culture, Native Americans, and lots of other subjects critical to an understanding of American history prior to 1877. *Writing the American Past* immerses readers in the documents, teaches them how to transcribe, decipher, and interpret primary sources, and offers a foundation and a template for understanding the American past and for developing lifelong interpretive skills. *Writing the American Past* is hands-on history. It brings key documents from American, British, and Canadian historical archives to you.

Primary Sources, Transcribing Sources

Primary sources are ordinarily sources written by contemporaries. Like secondary sources – those composed by people interpreting past events (such as historians) years later – they are influenced by, and reflect, larger contexts and forces. But unlike secondary sources, primary documents have an immediacy and liveliness that often captures the prevailing ideas and values of a person or a society at a particular time and in a particular place. This proximity is what constitutes the basic nature of primary evidence.

The dividends of working with primary sources generally are considerable and grant historians extraordinary access to a moment in time. Yet handwritten primary sources especially are often difficult to read, tricky to decipher, and sometimes challenging to interpret. Often, a handwritten primary source must be read several times and even then particular words and symbols will remain hazy or unclear. The historian might use several strategies to help him or her decipher documents. First and foremost, historians, through several readings, familiarize themselves with the document and thereby learn the idiom and style of the author and the geography of the document. Second, understanding the context in which the document was written can yield a great deal of information and often help the struggling eye identify the meaning of a particularly stubborn word or phrase. Lastly, historians, when stuck on a word they cannot decipher, often ask their colleagues for insight. Historians should never be reluctant to ask a fresh pair of eyes for their reading of especially troublesome words or sentences.

Once the document has been read and the majority of the text deciphered, historians often transcribe it either to clarify the content of the document for themselves or to make it available to other researchers. Their aim here is to provide readers with an accurate transcription, ideally with as little editorial intervention as possible. This is not to say that editorial intervention in the text is wholly undesirable. Seventeenth-, eighteenth-, and nineteenth-century conventions concerning capitalization and punctuation varied enormously and it is sometimes helpful for the person transcribing the document to standardize and edit it, provided they do not interfere with reading and understanding the document. Should the editor elect to employ this sort of silent editing, he or she needs to make a note to that effect so that the reader is not left with the impression that the transcription is an exact facsimile. Silent editing is often used when dealing with periods and dashes. Some writers used dashes to indicate a period while others used periods very sparingly. In such instances, silent editing is permissible provided, again, the editor or the transcriber indicates what they have done to change the text. Sometimes editors also provide annotations, usually in footnote or endnote form, in which they clarify the meaning of a word (especially if it is archaic) or provide details about a person or place mentioned in the text that is obscure.

Editors also employ various devices to indicate what they have changed, what they have left unchanged, and words or phrases they have omitted. The editorial use of the word *sic* (usually inserted into the transcription as [*sic*], the square brackets indicating that the editor has introduced the word or change) is used to show that a word in the original document that might appear incorrect or strange is, in fact, transcribed correctly and verbatim (*sic* may also be used if the original author of the document inadvertently wrote the same word twice). Occasionally, when an editor is at an absolute loss to decipher a particular word, he or she might insert either [?] or [illeg.] after the word to indicate that the transcription of the word or phrase is uncertain or illegible. Should the editor wish to indicate that his or her transcription omits a sentence or a string of words (perhaps for reasons of space limitations), ellipses may be employed as either [. . .] to show the omission of less than a sentence or [. . . .] to indicate the omission of a sentence or more.

An Example

Below is an example indicating some of the common editorial procedures outlined above. First, read the handwritten document itself and then examine how it has been transcribed and edited. The document is an extract of a letter written by John Basil Lamar, a southern planter and politician of Milledgeville, Georgia. The letter, written in 1835, is to his sister, Mary Ann Lamar, and it concerns his plantation, his slaves, and contains important clues indicating his view of the world.

Swift Creek, Jan'y 27th 1835

My Dear Sister

Yours dated 18th inst is now before me, on an old walnut side table, (which from its antique appearance, would warrant the belief that its commenced its career of usefulness, in the Lamar family at an early period. And as it successively groans under my nascent "bulletins," & "daily bread" (hog fowl, turnips &c) seems proud, that its last days, like its first, are to be spent, in the same family.) I took your letter from the office in Macon yesterday, & should have answer'd it forthwith, but preferring the calm of Swift Creek, to the boisterous crowd of the Central hotel, for that purpose, I deffer'd it until now.

I am more happy, Sister, than words can express, to learn, that you pass your time pleasantly, in Athens. You have "floated so long upon the tide of circumstances," and without having a home, you have had too many, Made from convenience and broken up from necessity. That I am extremely gratified to learn, that at lenght you are settled to your satisfaction, & that your new associates are to your taste & your visiters are pleasing, [....]

My new Carriage house, like an Arabs stable, is a part of my dwelling. I have converted one of my nice little shed rooms into that purpose, by sawing out a large door. My kitchen is in another shed room, I keep my ploughs, axes, hoes &c in the third, My overseer occupies one of the tenements of the main building, and I the hall. I have to regret that, there are no more shed rooms to my house, if there were Rob-roy, Redgauntlet & Kosciusko should then have a berth among us also, I have a garret to my house it, is true but it would incommode the rats, (who are lords paramount) overhead, as well as be somewhat inconvenient to the four footed gentry in getting up and down stairs.

My house, is a log castle of the first order, & I am as happy in it, as feudal baron, ever was, ensconsed in walls of stone. I will at some other time give you the geography & natural curiosities of my domain, they are interesting, I do assure you,

I am at present having my negro cabins refitted, and new ones built. Having consolidated my force on the north side of Swift Creek, I have an idea of <u>locating</u>, permanently on the south bank of that stream, where I have a snug white house, the house that father occupied, when on visits to the plantation.

Yours affectionately

John Basil, Lamar

Swift Creek, Jan'y 27th 1835

My Dear Sister

Yours dated 18th inst' is now before me, on an old walnut side table, (which from its antique appearance, would warrant the belief, that it commenced its career of usefulness, in the Lamar family, at an early period, and as it successively groans under my nascent "bulletins," & "daily bread" (hog fowl, turnips &c) seems proud, that its last days, like its first, are to be spent, in the same family.) I took your letter from the office in Macon yesterday, & should have answered it forthwith, but preferring the calm of Swift Creek, to the boisterous crowd of the Central hotel, for that purpose, I deffer'd it until now.

I am more happy, Sister, than words can express, to learn, that you have "floated, so long upon the tide of circumstances," and without having a home, you have had too many, made from convenience and broken up from necessity. What I am extremely gratified to learn, that at lenght [*sic*] you are settled to your satisfaction, & that your new associates are to your taste & your visitors are pleasing. [....]

My new carriage house, like an Arabs stable, is a part of my dwelling. I have converted one of my nice little shed rooms into that purpose, by sawing out a large door. My kitchen is in another shed room, I keep my ploughs, axes, hoes &c in the third, My overseer occupies one of the tenements of the main building, and I the hall. I have to regret that, there are no more shed rooms to my house, if there were Rob-roy,[1] Redgauntlet[2] & Kosciusko[3] should have a berth among us. Also, I have a garret to my house it is true but it would incommode the rats, (who are lords paramount) overhead, as well as be somewhat inconvenient to the four footed gentry in getting up and down stairs.

My house, is a log castle of the first order, & I am as happy in it, as feudal baron, ever was, ensconsed [*sic*] in walls of stone. I will at some other time give you the geography & natural curiosities of my domain, they are interesting, I do assure you.

I am at present having my negro cabins refitted, and new ones built. Having consolidated my force on the north side of Swift Creek, I have an idea of *locating*, permanently on the South bank of that stream, where I have a snug white house, the house that father occupied, when one visits to the plantation.

Yours affectionately
John Basil Lamar

The Collection

Writing the American Past reproduces 24 original documents and excerpts of documents detailing a variety of aspects and capturing a number of voices from the American past. Some are letters, others diary entries, still others financial documents, treaties, and official correspondence. Some are easy to decipher; others challenging, even very difficult. Some include conventions that will be largely unfamiliar to modern readers – old monetary systems, antiquated calendars, for example – and making sense of these conventions requires some research and perseverance. Largely missing from the selection are widely reprinted, previously transcribed, or particularly famous documents – such as the Gettysburg Address or the Constitution – simply because such documents defeat the purpose of the collection.

I have introduced each document to help readers place it in broad historical context and I have provided some specific details pertaining to each excerpt to help you better understand the document itself – who wrote it, when, and what it might tell us. But I have been careful not to divulge too much information about each document since the aim of each chapter is for you to engage the document fully, to interrogate it, decipher it, and then, finally, to interpret it. Each chapter also identifies the specifics of each document – its provenance, date, archival location – and also provides study questions to help you think about the significance of the document's contents. A list of suggested reading concludes each chapter.

Although many of the documents presented in this book can be read profitably in isolation, I have, at times, deliberately tried to tie together particular documents in an effort to suggest how history interrelates and braids. Where appropriate, I have suggested which documents connect.

Historical research is not easy and the art of reading primary, untranscribed documents is just that: an art. Not every scholar will transcribe the same document in precisely the same way and there will be disagreements over words and meanings. But the act of reading, transcribing, interpreting, and even disagreeing is an exciting enterprise, one that helps restore the full texture of the past, that helps the modern scholar engage with history, and which, ultimately, not only generates knowledge but invites scholars and historians to enter into serious conversations about the meaning of the past.

Notes

1 Robert Roy MacGregor, a well-known eighteenth-century Scottish folk hero.
2 Published in 1824, *Redgauntlet* was Sir Walter Scott's famous novel about the Jacobite cause. Scott was admired by southern planters for his veneration of the past.
3 The reference is very likely to Thaddeus Kosciusko (1746–1817), a Polish general revered by antebellum Americans for his role in support of the American Revolution.

Further Reading

Bloch, Mark 1964: *The Historian's Craft*. New York: Vintage.
Gaddis, John Lewis 2004: *The Landscape of History: How Historians Map the Past*. New York: Oxford University Press.
Kline, Mary-Jo 1998: *A Guide to Documentary Editing*. Baltimore, MD: The Johns Hopkins University Press.
Turabian, Kate L. 2007: *A Manual for Writers of Research Papers, Theses, and Dissertations*. Chicago: University of Chicago Press.

Chapter 1

Old World Explores New: Settling and Securing Newfoundland in the Early 1600s

Context

Why, beginning in the sixteenth and seventeenth centuries, did Europeans venture across the Atlantic Ocean and settle the Americas? Historians have offered several answers. Some stress the role of religion in promoting the so-called "Age of Discovery" and focus on the proselytizing efforts of the Spanish who in part aimed to "civilize" what they perceived as the "heathen" native peoples of Latin and South America in the ways of Catholicism. Other historians stress the larger context of the Renaissance in instigating European ventures in the Americas. Here, the Renaissance spirit of progress takes center-stage, an emphasis less on religion and more a general inquisitiveness, belief, and confidence in a nation's ability to grow and expand. Advances in navigation and shipbuilding, especially among the Portuguese, occupy an important place in this narrative. Expansion and colonization, aided by technological advancements, were, according to this interpretation, part and parcel of an adventurous spirit designed to bring glory to emerging European nation-states and monarchs.

Materialist explanations have also proven popular among some historians. Trade, material benefit, and wealth, so this argument goes, motivated various Europeans – the Spanish, Portuguese, Dutch, and English, among others – to mount the expensive ventures and military campaigns necessary to colonize the New World. Fear of want and uncertainty combined with anticipated riches – gold, furs, staples of various sorts – guided national thinking on expansion with both the merchant class and nobility invested in the success of the various ventures. European nations were often at odds in their competitive efforts to exploit the natural resources of the New World and colonization often took on a military overtone.

The effects of this Age of Discovery were multiple and enormous. Extremely diverse native peoples numbering over four million were often destroyed or severely weakened through disease or warfare and the development of precious plantation staples throughout the Americas led to the establishment of the slave trade, a trade responsible for the forced migration of over ten million Africans to the New World, 1450–1900. The quest for wealth led to the development of the "plantation complex" which, in turn, satisfied growing European demand for sugar, cacao, coffee, and tobacco, as well as a number of other foodstuffs. Modes and techniques of production and habits of consumption fed the Age of Discovery and helped establish its basic trajectory and form for over three hundred years.

In truth, and as many historians will agree, European colonization of the New World was influenced by many factors and it is likely that religious, economic, and cultural ideas worked together to inspire different nations at different times to embark on schemes to "discover" or exploit the New World. Moreover, the historian must pay attention to specifics if she or he is to divine why certain countries intervened in certain places at certain times in the New World. Place and time – context – matters and it is sometimes worthwhile examining places that frequently escape the attention of historians. While the exploration of the Caribbean, South America, and what later became the United States was certainly an important part of the Old World's encounter with the New, European settlement of colonies farther to the North – what later became Canada – was also important and revealing of motives and patterns behind settlement.

Variously referred to as "the new found land," "*terra de bacalhoa*," or "*terre neuve*," in the sixteenth century, Newfoundland was known to Europeans as early as the eleventh century when Greenlanders used northern Newfoundland as a temporary base for ship repair and as a starting point for the exploration of the Gulf of St. Lawrence. More systematic settlement had to wait several hundred years when the Venetian Zuan Caboto began to explore the eastern coast of the island in 1497. By the early 1500s, Europeans were busily harvesting Newfoundland's enormous cod reserves and shipping them back to Europe where demand for the fish was high. Records indicate that the first cargo of North American cod reached Bristol, England in 1502. Cod fishing – and, to a much lesser extent, whaling – drew Europeans to Newfoundland and proved critical to establishing economic ties between Old World and New. At first, a number of European nations fished the waters. Initially, especially by the 1540s, Norman and French Basque fishermen were central to the Newfoundland cod industry and they were joined by fishermen from the Basque coast of Spain in the 1540s. The English became more involved after the 1560s and by 1610 crews from the west coast of England and France came to dominate the trade. Numbers suggest the extent of the industry: 500 ships a year returned from Newfoundland by 1580 with various commodities, mostly cured cod. And with economic expansion came the slow but steady population of the region. By 1749 there were roughly 6,000 permanent settlers – some of them planters – connected to the fishing industry in Newfoundland.

Still, the number of migratory fishermen, those who came to fish off the Newfoundland coast in the summer and return to Europe with their salt-cured catches, vastly outnumbered the settlers. Yet the fishermen were to some extent dependent on the Newfoundland planters, relying on them to offer logistical support while fishing off the coast. Planters also relied on the migratory fishermen not least because the crews brought with them supplies and labor. But conflict between the two groups sometimes erupted. The fishermen and the planters often competed for shoreline space and there were also tensions between crews for that same land. Tension in Newfoundland sometimes echoed the political divisions emerging in England. The English Civil War of the 1640s, for example, divided Newfoundland settlers and reminded Newfoundlanders of their connection to the mother country. And the absence of a formal governing structure in Newfoundland – there was no effective local administration – hardly helped in resolving or containing the periodic conflicts. Later on, in the seventeenth century, stronger commercial ties with Massachusetts, which administered Newfoundland between 1651 and 1660, served to stabilize the island's economy and when Britain intervened in the colony's political life later in the eighteenth century, Newfoundland began to stabilize and enjoy greater formal protection from both pirates and the French.

The document presented here tends to support an older emphasis on the importance of trade and imperial policy in shaping the settlement of the Americas. Details concerning its author and even its date are sparse. The Library of Congress places the document in the rough range of 1611–1621 although there is some evidence internal to the text that it might have been written a little later. And although we do not know the author or authors, it seems reasonable to surmise that the document – excerpted here only in part – is of an official nature and addressed to British authorities. The document suggests the scope and importance of the cod trade to Britain and points to problems in maintaining it and realizing its full economic potential.

Source

Anonymous, "The Address and Reasons humbly offered for the speedy [settling] and [securing] of New found land, and the fishing trade there," Papers of David B. Quinn, Box 89, Folder 8, Research Files, New Foundland, Documents, Fishing Rights, 1611–1621, no date, Manuscript Division, Library of Congress, Washington, DC.

That Newfoundland hath time out of mind belonged to the Dominion of England and is the next part of the West Indies adjacent to his Majesties territories and lyes in equall degrees with Britany in France, and in the time of King James of blessed memory, there went yearely to fish there above 300 sayle of ships, wch did produce to this nation 500000 l p annm advantage, besides, the annuall education of 10000 Seamen, and brought into his majesties Revenew above 10000 l for Customes yearly by the product of the fish sent to Italy, France, Spaine, & Portugall, &c. for wch noething was Exported but pvisions, wch would have been soley consumed here att home to noe purpose, by the same psons, if they had not been imployed in that fishinge as by Sr Walter Rawleigh, and other worthey psons, assertions, and our dayly Experience will clearly appeare, & att this time there goes from England not above 60 sayle of shipps in a year to fish there, and in some late yeares not 20 sayle, and those make but small returnes, the reasons whereof as is humbly conceived are these that follow.

1 That there is noe harbour fortified to secure the mrchant from Pirats Sea Robers & Enemies.

2 That noe pportion of salt, nor other necessarye pvisions can be brought in, but from hand to mouth, wch often times spoyles their voyages, for in a good fishinge season the traders can imploy much more salt &c then they have by them.

3 That by reason noe settlement is made, all stages, Boats, traine fatts, flakes, and all manner of fishinge Craft, and stores are destroyed, either by the planters, or the first comers every season, by wch violent, and illegall actions, the fishermen are obleidged to a moneths delay, with the loss of all their more fishinge for soe longe and great labour, and charge to fit all things new, wch renders it soe excessive chargeable to the mrchants, & fishermen, that thereby forraigners undersell us in all marketts

[To the student: use this page to transcribe the text of the document on the opposite page]

Study Questions

1. How might we date this document? Are there clues suggesting when it could – and could not – have been written?
2. What is the purpose of the document?
3. What does the document suggest about the extent of the fishing industry in Newfoundland?
4. What were some of the specific problems facing migratory fishermen and how might they have been solved?
5. Based on this document, what do you consider to have been an important motivation for the expansion of European influence in the New World?

Further Reading

Abreu-Ferreira, D. 1998: Terra Nova through the Iberian Looking Glass: The Portuguese-Newfoundland Cod Fishery in the Sixteenth Century. 79 *Canadian Historical Review*, 100–15.

Cell, G. T. 1969: *English Enterprise in Newfoundland, 1577–1660*. Toronto: University of Toronto Press.

Cipolla, Carlo 1965: *Guns, Sails, and Empires: Technological Innovation and the Early Phase of European Expansion 1400–1700*. New York: Pantheon Books.

Crosby, Alfred 1972: *The Columbian Exchange: Biological and Cultural Consequences of 1492*. Westport, CT: Greenwood Press.

Curtin, Philip D. 1969: *The Atlantic Slave Trade: A Census*. Madison, WI: University of Wisconsin Press.

Elliott, J. H. 2006: *Empires of the Atlantic World: Britain and Spain in America 1492–1830*. New Haven and London: Yale University Press.

Innis, H. A. 1954: *The Cod Fisheries: The History of an International Economy*. Toronto: University of Toronto Press.

Mancall, Peter 1988: The Age of Discovery. 26 *Reviews in American History*, 26–53.

Pope, Peter 2003: Comparison: Atlantic Canada. In Daniel Vickers, ed., *A Companion to Colonial America*, Malden, MA: Blackwell Publishing, 489–507.

Pope, Peter 2004: *Fish into Wine: The Newfoundland Plantation in the Seventeenth Century*. Chapel Hill, NC: University of North Carolina Press.

Wright, Louis B. 1970: *Glory, Gold, and Gospel: The Adventurous Times of the Renaissance Explorers*. New York: Athenaeum.

Chapter 2

The Chesapeake: Indenturing Labor, 1694

Context

In 1617, Powhatan was the most powerful man on a bay some referred to as the Chesapeake. He was powerful because, by 1607, he was the head of an Indian confederacy numbering 9,000 who looked to him for stability. Powhatan had managed to minimize disputes among contending groups and thereby establish relative peace and prosperity.

After 1607 Powhatan had to take into account yet another "tribe" – they called themselves the "English." The English were a strange bunch. They had come to his world by sea, just over a hundred of them, dressed oddly and spoke strangely. They were foolish, too. When they first arrived, they followed a river deep into his territory and built a fort at a swampy, mosquito-infested place they called Jamestown. But the English did not worry Powhatan. They had boats and guns, to be sure, but he had learned how to use their firearms. Moreover, his confederacy vastly outnumbered them, and, since they had no women with them, how on earth could they thrive? Indeed, the English offered some benefits: they traded goods and, most importantly, their guns helped him quell resistance in his own confederacy. In addition, in 1614, Powhatan cemented his claim on the English with the marriage between his favorite child, Pocahontas, and an Englishman, John Rolfe. By 1617, all seemed right with Powhatan's world.

As Powhatan surveyed his empire, the King of England, James I did the same.

He was not pleased. While the Spanish were reaping gold and silver from their foothold in the New World, the English colonies in the Chesapeake and the Caribbean were struggling. Both suffered from high mortality, labor shortages, and a general sense of uncertainty. This was not supposed to be. The colonies operated according to an economic theory coined "mercantilism," a system of political economy designed to increase the wealth of the nation by fostering a favorable balance of trade. In an effort to bring his colonies into line, to make them economically worthwhile, James I set about trying to make English colonization in America profitable. In 1606 he granted a charter to several English merchants, gentlemen, and aristocrats, and they in turn founded the Virginia Company of London. The members of the Virginia Company sold stock to investors and awarded a share in the Company to those who were willing to settle in Virginia at their own expense. With the proceeds from the sale of the stock, the Company planned to send to the Chesapeake hundreds of poor and unemployed people as well as scores of skilled craftsmen, many of whom were to serve the Company seven years in return for their passage. These indentured servants were the labor designed to bolster the fledgling colony.

Success was slow and uneven. Many workers were indolent – understandably so given the high rate of debilitating malaria – and in 1618 more sweeping and effective reforms were imposed in an effort to attract more capital and colonists from England. The Virginia Company established a "headright" system that granted land to individuals. Those who had already settled received one hundred acres a piece; new settlers got fifty; anyone who paid the passage of other immigrants to Virginia was allocated fifty acres per "head." The Company allowed the planters to elect a general assembly – the House of Burgesses – in 1619 and, partly as a result of these measures, more settlers came to the colony in the 1620s.

The settlers were mainly working men and some women, generally young (typically 15–24), and came because they perceived that their prospects were better in Virginia than in England. Even though three-quarters of all immigrants who arrived in the Chesapeake did so as indentured servants who had to work for a given number of years before they became "free" (indenture terms were typically five to seven years), they came because, in the long term, they might be able to grow the profitable crop of tobacco, an alluring prospect given their life of poverty in England. But indentured servants faced many problems, problems that the sponsors of migration tended to gloss over in their promotional literature. The death rate in Virginia in the 1620s was higher than that of England (life expectancy for Chesapeake men who reached the age of 20 was 48 years) and servants fared worst of all. As planters scrambled to make a quick profit, they extracted the maximum amount of labor from their servants and, as a result, 40 percent of them did not survive to the end of their indenture.

After the tumultuous decade of the 1620s and following James's decision to revoke the Virginia Company charter, thus rendering Virginia a Royal Colony administered by the Crown via a Governor, conditions began to settle. The planters consolidated political power under Royal administration and began to impose some order on social and political life. The stability also brought benefits for servants – they were no longer exploited as quickly, mortality rates declined, food reserves increased, and most managed to outlive their indentures with enough money to become small planters themselves.

Yet Virginia was in some ways hurt by its own success. As its inhabitants started to live longer, more servants survived their terms; once free, they set up as tobacco planters. With more planters, the production of tobacco increased, sending prices downward, especially between 1660 and 1680. To maintain profits, they had to produce more tobacco, which meant that the biggest planters bought up more land on the coast. Smaller farmers had to move inland and this often led to increased conflict with Native Americans. The downward spiral in tobacco prices also meant that more small farmers went into debt, especially in the 1660s, and some even reassumed indentured servitude. The elite were worried and attempted to contain conflict by curbing the political rights of landless men and even lengthening the terms of indentures. Their efforts failed and in 1676 civil war erupted in Virginia in the form of Bacon's Rebellion, pitting poor and middling against rich. Although the Rebellion eventually collapsed, it alerted Virginia's elites to the dangers of class warfare and the problems with indentured white servants.

Partly as a result of Bacon's Rebellion, at the end of the 1600s Virginia planters began to slowly move away from a reliance on indentured servants. Other factors facilitated the transition. First, there were simply fewer young people in England willing to become indentured servants. Toward the end of the century, England enjoyed a rise in real wages and a drop in the birth rate, which effectively limited the supply of white servants and resulted in a 20 percent decrease in the number of white migrants headed for Virginia in the years 1680–99. Even more importantly, Virginia began to move toward a race-based system of slavery which viewed Africans as natural slaves. This shift was very protracted. Although the first Africans had been brought to Virginia by the Dutch in 1619 and while the 1640s witnessed the introduction of a number of laws that helped institute the system of legal slavery, relatively few Africans were enslaved. Even by 1670, there were only about 2,000 blacks in Virginia, just about 5 percent of the population. But the decrease in the supply of white servants and the fears associated with class warfare led gradually, by the early 1700s, to the adoption of a policy of the presumption of servitude for Africans who were increasingly enslaved *durante vita*, or for life. Planters began to invest more heavily in slaves than in indentured servants because declining mortality rates for slaves made them more profitable. As a result, the Chesapeake changed from a society based on temporary white servitude to permanent black slavery. By 1740, 40 percent of all Virginians were black and most were African-born.

Among the most important effects of this shift was a growing unity based on race in Virginia society so that color – whiteness specifically – meant power and served to lessen the class tensions within white society. This racialization of enslaved labor held momentous implications for American history, as we will see in several of the chapters that follow.

Source

Assignment of indenture, dated 21 March 1694, of Thomas Gibson, of Whitehaven, United Kingdom, to Thomas Spencer, for seven years. Recorded in Middlesex County, Virginia, 2 April 1694, by Richard Filbeck. The Library of Virginia, Richmond, Virginia.

I assigned to mr Thomas Spencer a Lad came in this yeare in the Shipp Rainbow from White haven named Thomas Gibson for Seaven yeare next to come after this Date. Witness my name this 21th of March 1693/4

Witness Richd Willis

At a Court held for ye County of Midd[x] ye 2d day of Apr. 1694

Richd Willis

[illegible] Mickleborough

Then appeared mr Thomas Spencer & Acknowledged the above Assignment in open Court

Test Edwin Thacker Clr

[To the student: use this page to transcribe the text of the document on the opposite page]

Study Questions

1. What are the terms of this indenture?
2. What is the date of the document? Is there something peculiar about it?
3. Who benefited from this indenture and why?

Further Reading

Carr, Lois Green 1992: Emigration and the Standard of Living: The Seventeenth Century Chesapeake. *Journal of Economic History* 52, 271–92.

Galenson, David W. 1981: *White Servitude in Colonial America: An Economic Analysis*. Cambridge and New York: Cambridge University Press.

Gleach, Frederic W. 1997: *Powhatan's World and Colonial Virginia: A Conflict of Cultures*. Lincoln, NE: University of Nebraska Press.

Greene, Jack P. 1988: *Pursuits of Happiness: The Social Development of Early Modern British Colonies and the Formation of American Culture*. Chapel Hill, NC: University of North Carolina Press.

Isaac, Rhys 1982: *The Transformation of Virginia, 1740–1790*. Chapel Hill, NC: University of North Carolina Press, 1982.

Kulikoff, Allan 1986: *Tobacco and Slaves: The Development of Southern Cultures in the Chesapeake, 1680–1800*. Chapel Hill, NC: University of North Carolina Press.

Kupperman, Karen O. 2007: *The Jamestown Project*. Cambridge, MA: Belknap Press.

Morgan, Philip D. 1998: *Slave Counterpoint: Black Culture in the Eighteenth-Century Chesapeake and Lowcountry*. Chapel Hill, NC: University of North Carolina Press.

Woolley, Benjamin 2007: *Savage Kingdom: The True Story of Jamestown, 1607, and the Settlement of America*. New York: Harper Collins.

Chapter 3

Life in Seventeenth-century New England: Massachusetts in the 1690s

Context

Whatever problems plagued the Chesapeake, it looked, to some English eyes at least, a far better place to colonize than the stony, cold ground of New England, which had no minerals to mine and no crops suitable for export. By the 1620s, however, economic, political, and religious developments in England made New England look increasingly hospitable, at least from some quarters.

When he assumed the throne from Elizabeth I in 1603, James I vowed to purge England of all radical Protestant reformers. He had in mind the Puritans, most of whom were Presbyterians or Congregationalists. Despite some theological differences, both believed in predestination, namely that God had ordained the outcome of history and of every human being. Puritans found comfort in predestination and strove to play their part in the drama and discover in their performance some signs of personal salvation. Predestination called for reforming both church and society along Calvinist lines and the Puritans thought that England's government hampered religious purity and social order because it tolerated drunkenness, gambling, extravagance, Catholicism, and Sabbath breaking. Many Puritans believed that the Church of England was too corrupt to be reformed and they abandoned Anglican worship, meeting secretly in small congregations. Persecuted by the government, by 1608 enough of them were discouraged to leave England and they migrated to Holland where they hoped to find some degree of religious freedom. They were disappointed and ultimately decided to move again to the New World, specifically to Virginia. A series of navigational mistakes in the *Mayflower* landed them far to the north of the Chesapeake and in November 1620, 88 Separatist "Pilgrims" set anchor at a place they called Plymouth in southeast Massachusetts. Aided by local Native Americans, their own ability to establish a rudimentary form of government, and a general indifference toward their presence by English authorities, these men and women of relatively modest means managed to establish a small but increasingly stable society.

These Pilgrims were joined by a second wave of Puritan migrants in the 1620s who, in 1629, organized the Massachusetts Bay Company and, even though they were disliked by the Crown, managed to obtain a royal charter confirming their title to the colony. Generally of a higher class and wealthier than the first settlers, the second wave of migrants held a strong sense of mission and destiny. They did not think of themselves as abandoning the English church but, rather, saw their relocation to the New World as a regrouping for another assault on corruption. Their advance parties established Salem township and in 1630 the Company's first governor, John Winthrop – a landed gentleman and lawyer – became the colony's chief executive. He helped establish a charter by which every male adult church member was allowed to participate in the colony's governance.

New England proved more hospitable to the English than the Chesapeake for several reasons. First, New England settlers tended to arrive in family groups and so the colony avoided many of the problems associated with dispossessed indentured servants. Moreover, New England settlers were largely skilled workers, often literate, enjoyed a more balanced sex ratio than settlers in Virginia, and shared a common past of persecution in England, giving the group a solidarity missing in the Chesapeake and enabling them to achieve a relatively stable society more quickly.

Efforts to establish structure characterized much of New England's early history. They tended to live in tight-knit communities, almost every adult male owned property, and the nature of the region's economy meant that while there was social stratification, the distance between rich and poor was not as great as in the Chesapeake. On the whole, New England, although engaged in the trans-Atlantic trade, tended to strive for sufficiency primarily and was less involved in the export of staples. Congregational churches were also important for helping to stabilize New England society. Many settlers formed churches quickly as they founded towns and each congregation ran its own affairs. Although membership was voluntary it was not available for the asking and those wishing to join the church had to persuade church authorities that they had experienced a "conversion" – a turning of the heart and soul toward God, a spiritual rebirth reflected in a pious and disciplined life. All of this tended to give New England communities a sense of order.

None of this is to suggest that New England was not without its conflicts or tensions and not every group benefited from the tight New England social structure. Women, for example, tended to have little scope or freedom. Most adult women were hardworking farmwives who cared for large households. Between marriage and middle age many were pregnant. They tended to be housebound (men traveled to market) and they suffered legal disadvantages as well – with very few exceptions they had little or no control over property. Wives could not sue and could not make contracts. Divorce was virtually impossible. Only widows and a few single women had the same property rights as a man. For the most part, women held the status of a "helpmeet" – a chaste, submissive wife and mother who served God by serving man.

In fact, conflicts in New England arose in part at least precisely because people were so tightly bound in their web of social relations. Historians have frequently focused on these ruptures and to good profit. Perhaps most infamously, a great deal of attention has been paid to the Salem witchcraft trials of 1692 in which nineteen people were hanged for suspicion of practicing witchcraft. The majority of those executed were older, middle-aged women, mostly widows with property. In other words, there is some evidence to suggest that it was precisely those women who transgressed the status of helpmeet that were identified as witches which, in turn, suggests a degree of intolerance of female independence.

While historians have been correct to focus on the witchcraft trials specifically and the stratified nature of New England society generally, such an emphasis can obscure the more mundane – and arguably more typical – aspects of daily life in New England. Witchcraft trials and religious disputes were not the norm. Rather, people muddled through and tried as best they could to survive in a time and place that could be fairly unforgiving. Reproduced here is an excerpt from the diary of John Marshall of Braintree, Massachusetts, who was the clerk of Captain Thomas Savage's Braintree company. Marshall typically describes current events in the community, many of which seem banal and his "Remarks on August 1697" are no exception. Yet it is the very ordinariness of his observations that grants us access to what was important to the average person and suggests something about the texture of daily life. Moreover, not all of Marshall's comments describe tedious events. Some, by the standards of the time, are exciting, even though they have nothing to do with witches or religious tension.

Source

"Remarks on August 1697" and "May 1699," John Marshall Diary, 1689–1711, P-363, reel 6.22 (microfilm), Ms. N-1626, Massachusetts Historical Society, Boston, Massachusetts.

Remarke on August 1697:

Allthough in the Last month we had some small showers of Rain wherby the corn was preserved from perishing wholly: yet ther had not been a soaking plentifull Rain since the month of may till the 3d of this month: and then it Rained moderatly most part of the Day and all the night following it Rained most plentifully. insomuch that Rivers and Brooks rise very considerably by reason therof: a very great mercy the sabbath before the first Chh in Boston agreed to keep thirsday following as a day of fasting and prayr to aske Rain. the mercy came before the Day came: But it was kept accordingly:

on the 11 of this month a new ship: of or about 300 tuns Burthen lying near the shoar in Boston Loading and fittinge for the sea. By some accident took fire and was Burned the whole Loss was severall thousands of pounds

[To the student: use this page to transcribe the text of the document on the opposite page]

Study Questions

1. List the main themes or issues that Marshall notes in his diary entry.
2. How, if at all, was daily life connected to religious belief?
3. Can we surmise anything about the importance of trade to Massachusetts from this document?

Further Reading

Boyer, Paul and Stephen Nissenbaum 1974: *Salem Possessed: The Social Origins of Witchcraft*. Cambridge, MA: Harvard University Press.

Daniels, Bruce C. 2005: *Puritans at Play: Leisure and Recreation in Colonial New England*. New York: Palgrave Macmillan.

Greven Jr., Philip J. 1970: *Four Generations: Population, Land, and Family in Colonial Andover, Massachusetts*. Ithaca, NY: Cornell University Press.

Johnson, Claudia Durst 2002: *Daily Life in Colonial New England*. Westport, CT: Greenwood Press.

Karlsen, Carol F. 1987: *The Devil in the Shape of Woman: Witchcraft in Colonial New England*. New York: W. W. Norton.

Lockridge, Kenneth A. 1985: *A New England Town: The First One Hundred Years*. New York: W. W. Norton.

Main, Gloria L. 2004: *Peoples of a Spacious Land: Families and Cultures in Colonial New England*. Cambridge, MA: Harvard University Press.

Stout, Harry S. 1988: *The New England Soul: Preaching and Religious Culture in Colonial New England*. New York: Oxford University Press.

Ulrich, Laurel Thatcher 1982: *Good Wives: Image and Reality in the Lives of Women in Northern New England, 1650–1750*. New York: Alfred A. Knopf.

Chapter 4

The Middle Colonies: A Philadelphia Furrier, 1738

Context

Traditionally, historians have characterized what is now New York, Pennsylvania, Delaware, and New Jersey as the middle colonies. On the whole, settlers in the middle colonies tended to lead more secure lives than southern colonists even as they lacked the common bonds that lent stability to New England. The middle colonies were extremely ethnically and religiously diverse, drawing settlers from the Netherlands and England especially, as well as having significant German, Scotch-Irish, Swedish, Belgian, Portuguese, French, Finnish, and African populations. The Dutch influence was particularly apparent in New York and New Jersey and Germans, mainly from the Rhineland, were an important presence in Pennsylvania. These colonies were, in other words, characterized by plurality and ethnic heterogeneity. They were also economically robust, and increasingly so. Typically, the middle colonies exported surplus foodstuffs – wheat, livestock, and barley – to West Indian plantations and the fur trade in New York was especially important to the region's economic life. As a result, Philadelphia came to eclipse Boston as the largest city in colonial America.

The Dutch influence in New York was felt most keenly early on in the colony's history. New York was settled in 1624 as New Netherlands – an outpost of the Dutch West India Company. The Dutch hold in New York was, by design, tenuous. More impressed with the commercial potential of Africa and South America, the Dutch limited their investment in New York to a few posts catering to the fur trade. Because they were interested principally in trade, the Dutch had little desire to plant permanent colonies. The few initial Dutch settlers clustered in the village of New Amsterdam on Manhattan Island and up the Hudson River at a trading post, Fort Orange (now Albany).

A number of ethnicities coexisted with the Dutch in the New Netherlands. It was also at times quite an unstable colony, plagued by various religious and ethnic disputes and there was tension with Native Americans in some areas. Conflict with Native Americans especially had long term implications for the middle colonies. Generally, Native American groups of the middle colonies and New York were stronger than in other parts of colonial North America and one group in particular – the Iroquois – became more powerful, at least temporarily, as a result of the white presence. The key to the Iroquois' success lay in their ability to exploit the fur trade. Early on, the Native Americans of northern New York became important suppliers of furs to European traders and because they far outnumbered white settlers, the handful of Dutch and English had every reason to keep peace with them. But as elsewhere in colonial America, the fur trade heightened tensions between New York Indian tribes. At first, the Mahicans had supplied furs to the Dutch but by 1625 the game in their territory had been exhausted and the Dutch took their business to the Iroquois. When the Iroquois faced the same extinction of fur-bearing animals in the 1640s, they found a solution: with Dutch guns, the Iroquois attempted to eliminate their competition with neighboring tribes (notably the Huron) and seized their hunting grounds. The destruction of the Huron made the Iroquois the undisputed power on the northern frontier and gave them considerable power, so much so that European settlers in the region had to often tread carefully and deal diplomatically with the Iroquois and affiliated tribes.

In 1654, the Dutch West India Company went bankrupt and virtually abandoned its American colony. The English King, Charles II, took advantage of the collapse and granted the Duke of York (James, his brother) a proprietary charter covering the New Netherlands territory. In 1664 the English invaded, the remaining Dutch officials surrendered, and New Amsterdam was renamed New York. The English administration of the colony did little to resolve ethnic tensions or promote political harmony. The remaining Dutch resented English rule and only after a generation of intermarriage, cultural adaptation, and creolization did tension begin to fade and the colony take on a more English cultural hue. All told, even by 1698, economic and urban growth was still modest. New York City had barely 18,000 people by this date and it was only in the next century that it became an important colony.

If New York and New Jersey might best be characterized by their ethnic diversity and relatively unsettled conditions, Pennsylvania was quite different. The colony shared a religious and political idealism similar to New England and the heavy German and Quaker presence gave it a general consistency, although the colony would become quite diverse with the arrival of the Scots-Irish in the eighteenth century. The key figure was William Penn, the colony's founder, a Quaker and leader in the Society of Friends. Penn envisioned his North America colony as a refuge for English Quakers (who in return would pay him taxes) and he actively publicized the colony settlement and distributed pamphlets throughout England and Europe. It worked: by 1700 Pennsylvania's population stood at 21,000 and it grew quickly.

About half of Pennsylvania's settlers arrived as indentured servants; the other half were farmers and artisans. These experienced settlers brought skills with them that contributed to the colony's economic growth. Farmers made excellent use of the region's rich soil and attained not only a degree of self-sufficiency but also frequently exported some agricultural products, wheat especially, to the Caribbean. Moreover, relations with coastal Indians (the Delaware) were generally cordial not least because the Quakers posed no threat to them. Because the Quakers were committed to pacifism and because they believed that the Indians rightfully owned their own land, a general peace prevailed. Indeed, before Penn sold land to white settlers, he bought it from the Delaware. He also prohibited the sale of alcohol to Indians and regulated the fur trade to prevent disputes. Pennsylvania, then, was, generally speaking, a relatively stable colony, one with freedom of worship, basic English civil liberties, and one that tended to attract colonists and settlers.

It was not Elysium, of course, and there were tensions, principally between Penn and his allies – mostly large landowners and his friends – and common farmers who opposed the elite's efforts to control political initiatives and to collect taxes on their lands. Tension was sufficiently high that some counties with a preponderance of non-Quaker farmers (the Lower Counties) agitated to separate. Penn, though, managed to buy peace by revising the colony's structure of government and in 1701 Pennsylvania adopted the Charter of Privileges – in effect, a new constitution, limiting the power of the elite, Penn's privileges as proprietor, and empowering the colony's farming interests.

This political recalibration helped the colony prosper, so much so that in the eighteenth century it became home to colonial America's commercial and cultural center: Philadelphia. Generally, cities in colonial America were modest affairs, at least measured in terms of population (90 percent of colonial Americans lived outside of urban areas). Yet cities exercised an important influence on the culture and, especially, the commerce of colonial America and Philadelphia became the preeminent city in North America during the eighteenth century. With 30,000 people by the end of the colonial period, the only larger city in the British Empire was London (New York's population stood at 25,000, Boston's was 16,000).

The document presented here – excerpts from a 1738 account book kept by a Philadelphia furrier, Samuel Neave – is suggestive of several features of the city, its culture, and the region generally. First, note the man's trade – he dealt in furs. Here, we see evidence of the connection between countryside and town, between the frontier economies of the fur trade and the consumer economy of Philadelphia. The account book lists the type of furs with which Neave worked and their cost and it suggests something about the supply of furs and demand for finished fur garments. Second, note where Neave keeps his accounts – in an almanac. Essential for farmers and city dwellers alike, colonial almanacs offered a wealth of often scientific information about time, dates, the history of weather patterns, predictions about the year, and they were often peppered with poetry, witticisms, and choice pieces of advice. Often associated with the growing Enlightenment in colonial America – the triumphing of reason and science over superstition – almanacs helped people think about their worlds in a structured, generally logical fashion. This document also indicates some of the challenges of performing historical research. The volume is bound so tightly that not every piece of information – especially Neave's list of debts – can be read. Such is the nature of historical research and it is the historian's job to make sense as best as she or he can of documents that are sometimes reluctant to surrender all of their information.

Source

Samuel Neave, account, kept in his copy of *Bradford's almanac for 1738* (Am.1075), The Historical Society of Pennsylvania, Philadelphia, Pennsylvania.

Acct. Furrs Bt. 1737

Date	Item	Rate	£	s	d
Jan. 5th	√ 14 Racoon Skins	14d	=	16	4
	√ 5 Fox	2/	=	10	=
Jany 1st	√ 12 Racoons	16d	=	16	=
	√ 3 Fox	2/	=	6	=
	√ 2 Minks	15d	=	2	6
30th	√ 5 Racoons	@ 16d	=	6	8
	√ 3 Fox	@ 2/4	=	7	=
	√ 1 Cat		=	2	=
	√ 2 Musk Ratts		=	=	4
31	√ 18 Racoon	@ 17d	1	5	6
	√ 9 Fox	@ 2/5	1	1	9
	√ 1 Catt	@	=	2	5
	√ 5 Minks	@ 16d	=	6	8
	√ 1 do	@	=	=	=
	√ 3 Musk Ratts		=	=	6
Feb. 3	√ 10 Racoons		=	9	6
	√ 2 Fox		=	1	=
	√ 1 Catt		=	=	6
	√ 1 Otter		=	2	6
7th	√ 15 Racoon	@ 16d	1	=	=
	√ 6 Fox	2/	=	12	=
	√ 2 Cat		=	4	=
	√ 5 Mink	16d	=	6	8
[illegible]	in Wastebook		£8	19	10

[To the student: use this page to transcribe the text of the document on the opposite page]

List of Old Debts. £ S D

Name	£	S	D
Ann Caney	9	14	1
Brian O'Neel Knots	2	16	
Thomas Pratt	3		
Mary Peirce	5	4	
Cathr. Stapler	4	16	
Ann Godfrey	4	18	
Caleb Cash	1	13	
Saml. Wright	5	7	
Chris. Topham	8	6	
Ralph Ashton	1	7	
Luke Sheeld		15	
John Holland	7	12	
James Fox Note hand	41		
Geo: Reese Jones	1	16	
Wid. Campion	2	15	
Jacob Gooding	6	7	
John Johnson	3	11	
Benjn. VanBurkeloo	3	5	
Thos. Mitchell	2	3	
Elias Cotting	48	12	
4 Thos. Prior	3	16	
Frederick Elbershat	28	17	

Pensilvania, 1738.

AN

ALMANACK,

OR

EPHEMERIS

Of the daily Motions of the SUN *and* MOON;

The time of their Rising and Setting. Lunations *and* Eclipses.

With the

Places and Aspects of the Planets,

Exactly Calculated for the Year 1738.

Being from the	*Years*
Building of London	2845
Building of Rome	2490
Beginning of the Julian Year	1791
Destruction of Jerusalem *and* 1337490 Jews	1668
Invention of PRINTING	278
Birth of Copernicus	265
Beginning of the Gregorian Year	166
Burning of London	72
Royal Grant of Pensilvania	57
Arrival of the Proprietary THOMAS PENN	6

By Jacob Taylor.

For Earth has this variety from Heaven,
Of Pleasure situate in Hill and Dale. *Milton.*
And now my Muse what most delights her sees,
A living Gallery of aged trees;
In such green Palaces the first Kings reign'd,
Slept in their shades and Angels entertain'd. Waller.

Philadelphia: *Printed and Sold by* Andrew Bradford, *at the Sign of the* Bible; *Sold also by* John Taylor *at* Concord, *&* *by several Shopkeepers in Town & Country.*

[To the student: use this page to transcribe the text of the document on the opposite page]

Study Questions

1. You have already encountered references to "pounds" but this document lists money in a way that might be unfamiliar to you. What is the "system" being used and how did it work?
2. Suggest the significance of Neave's decision to keep his accounts in an almanac.
3. What can we deduce about the nature of Neave's trade from these brief excerpts?
4. What sort of information does the almanac contain and is there anything about dates and time that might require some explanation?

Further Reading

Balmer, Randall H. 1989: *A Perfect Babel of Confusion: Dutch Religion and English Culture in the Middle Colonies*. New York: Oxford University Press.

Bauman, Richard 1971: *For the Reputation of Truth: Politics, Religion, and Conflict among the Pennsylvania Quakers, 1750–1800*. Baltimore, MD: The Johns Hopkins University Press.

Doerflinger, Thomas M. 2001: *A Vigorous Spirit of Enterprise: Merchants and Economic Development in Revolutionary Philadelphia*. Chapel Hill, NC: University of North Carolina Press.

Jacobsen, Douglas G. 1991: *An Unprov'd Experiment: Religious Pluralism in Colonial New Jersey.* New York: Carlson Publishing.

Nash, Gary B. 1968: *Quakers and Politics: Pennsylvania, 1681–1726*. Princeton, NJ: Princeton University Press.

Offutt, William M. 1995: *Of "Good Laws" and "Good Men": Law and Society in the Delaware Valley, 1680–1710*. Urbana, IL: University of Illinois Press.

Tolles, Frederick B. 1948: *Meeting House and Counting House: The Quaker Merchants of Colonial Philadelphia, 1682–1763*. Chapel Hill, NC: University of North Carolina Press.

Wolf, Stephanie Grauman 1976: *Urban Village: Population, Community, and Family Structure in Germantown, Pennsylvania, 1683–1800*. Princeton, NJ: Princeton University Press.

Chapter 5

The Lower South and Slave Society: Slave Resistance and Imperial Contests, 1739

Context

Since the sixteenth century, an imperial battle had raged in the Caribbean between England and Spain over who would control the islands. Distracted by developments on the mainland and unable to invest the necessary resources, by the early 1600s Spain began to lose some – though, as we shall see, by no means all – of its influence in the area. The English as well as the Dutch and French began to fill the vacuum. The English saw the Caribbean as another colonial outpost not unlike Virginia. Between 1604 and 1644 about 30,000 immigrants from Britain moved to the Caribbean, particularly to the islands of St. Kitts, Barbados, and Nevis. Some of these early settlers, predominantly young men, were free, some indentured. At first, they cultivated a very poor quality tobacco and lived pretty wretched lives. Conditions improved for the British Caribbean, however, with the introduction of sugar cultivation, especially in Barbados. The staple transformed the Caribbean and the British West Indies.

Even though planters in the British West Indies ranked among the richest people in English America throughout the seventeenth century it was riddled with disease and island populations grew only minimally. Smaller farmers were squeezed for land as the big planters expanded in their quest for more profit. Increased sugar production led to another threat: huge increases in black slaves to cultivate the staple. By the beginning of the eighteenth century, slaves outnumbered white residents by four to one and with the increase came white fear of servile insurrection. White authorities responded with draconian slave codes and laws but lived under constant siege and fear and during the first century of settlement, several major slave uprisings took place in the British West Indies. As land became scarce and revolts became increasingly likely, some planters began to look for alternatives and it was this search for new prospects that linked the history of the British West Indies to the southern mainland colonies.

Another important development shaping the settlement of the southern colonies came from the schemes of William Berkeley, Virginia's Royal Governor during Bacon's Rebellion, and Sir John Colleton, a Caribbean planter. Colleton saw that the Caribbean had a surplus of white settlers and Berkeley believed that Virginia needed to expand. They convinced Charles II to make them joint proprietors in 1663 of a place they called the Carolinas. North Carolina was established as a colony in 1701 and it produced mainly agricultural goods and some naval stores – masts, pitch, tar, turpentine.

The southern portion of the Carolinas held far more promise, especially for one of its big supporters and proprietors, Sir Anthony Ashley Cooper (the Earl of Shaftesbury). In 1669 he sponsored an expedition of a few hundred settlers from England, Virginia, and Barbados to plant the first permanent settlement in South Carolina. By 1680 they had founded Charles Town (later Charleston) at the confluence of the Cooper and Ashley Rivers. Cooper tried to lure settlers by touting the navigable rivers and offering liberal land grants, religious toleration, and a representative government. The new settlers would enrich Cooper and the other proprietors by paying quitrents.

Cooper hoped more than simply to create a settlement, however – his aims were for something better, a sort of ideal society – but this would not be realized for white settlers until the colony found profitable export crops. Initially, South Carolinians raised grains and cattle that they exported to the West Indies. They then diversified into trade in deerskins in collaboration with coastal Native American tribes such as the Yamasee and the Creek and the Catawba of the interior. As elsewhere in colonial America, this trade caused some tension both between Native Americans and white settlers, with wrangles over indebtedness and Indian dependence on guns, rum, and clothing. In 1715 white settlers found themselves involved in a serious conflict – the Yamasee War – that for a time threatened the future of the colony.

Rice cultivation changed everything. By the beginning of the eighteenth century, it was the colony's chief export staple and the returns for planters were fabulous. The constant demand for rice from Europe made South Carolina an extraordinarily rich colony and the planters of the low country some of the wealthiest people in North America. Although the Crown assumed control of the colony in 1729, economically at least, South Carolina prospered and achieved a semblance of stability.

And yet the source of that economic security – rice – was also a source of social instability simply because planters increasingly employed slaves to cultivate the difficult crop. Earlier in the colony's history, the black population had enjoyed a degree of freedom, particularly when labor was scarce. Some even served in the militia, defending against attacks from Native Americans and the Spanish to the south. But as the number of black slaves increased in the seventeenth century, whites, as they did elsewhere, clamped down on these freedoms in an effort to control the burgeoning slave population. The quest for financial gain compromised the colony's security: more rice meant greater profit which, in turn, necessitated using more slaves, whose very numbers seemed to overwhelm the colony's white settlers. By 1708 black men and women were the racial majority in South Carolina; by 1730 they outnumbered whites two to one.

Imperial struggles in the Lower South hardly eased the problem in South Carolina. Although the establishment of Georgia in 1752 served to help secure South Carolina's southern border, the increased activities of the Spanish in Florida – still held by the Spanish Empire – threatened the short- and long-term security of the colony. Spain founded St. Augustine in 1565 as a small colonial outpost. Even by 1700 it had about only 1,500 people, mostly black slaves, Indians, and Catholic missionaries. It was principally a religious colony, designed to teach the "natives" the virtues of Catholicism, and an outpost from which to antagonize the British Empire to the north. To achieve both aims, in the seventeenth century, the Spanish offered freedom to any escaped slaves willing to defend the colony and convert to Catholicism. Black fugitives from South Carolina especially (Georgia initially banned slavery, although it later relented) fled in some numbers and established a settlement made up principally of former slaves just north of St. Augustine at Gracia Real de Santa Teresa de Mose. This served as a post against British expansion and as a base for raiding the Carolinas and Georgia.

Although the outpost was small, it proved problematic for both Georgia and South Carolina. By escaping to Spanish Florida, slaves participated not only in their own liberation but also in the intricate machinations of imperial encounter between Spain and England in North America. Sometimes, in fact, slave action threatened the stability of South Carolina in profound ways. In September 1739, for example, dozens of enslaved black South Carolinians initiated an insurrection in their effort to escape en masse to Florida – known as the Stono Rebellion – and, in the process, confirmed to South Carolina authorities just how precarious their slave society was and how slaves and the Spanish offer of freedom could threaten it in substantive ways. White authorities in South Carolina and Georgia had encountered sporadic efforts along these lines before and barely three months prior to the Stono insurrection – arguably the largest revolt in colonial mainland North America's history – William Bull, South Carolina's acting Governor, had written to British authorities in London warning of the difficulties posed by the Spanish and the effect their offer of freedom was having on slaves. Part of that document is reprinted here and it serves to remind us not only of the imperial, transatlantic aspects of the Lower South's history but also of the ability of slaves to initiate action and to read aspects of the political geography of imperial contest in the region. The document suggests just how susceptible white South Carolina was to action by its black majority, a black majority they had created in the quest for economic profit.

Source

William Bull, Charleston, SC, to His Grace the Duke of New Castle, 9 May 1739, Records in the British Public Records Office Relating to South Carolina, 1711–82 (Sainsbury Transcripts), vol. 20, pp. 185–6, South Carolina Department of Archives and History, Columbia, SC (C.O. Papers, S.C. Original Correspondence, Secretary of State, 1730–46, No. 5/388).

South Carolina the 9th May 1739.

My Lord

I beg leave to lay before your Grace an affair, Which may greatly distress, if not intirely ruin, this His Majestys Province of South Carolina.

His Catholick Majestys Edict having been published At St. Augustine, declaring Freedom, to all Negroes, and Other Slaves, that shall desert from the English Colonies, Has occasioned several parties to desert from this Province both by Land and Water, which notwithstanding They were pursued by the People of Carolina as well as The Indians, & People in Georgia by General Oglethorpes Directions, have been able to make their escape.

To prevent the like attempts, as far as was in the Power of this Government Deputys have been sent To St. Augustine, to demand the restitution of these Deserters, pursuant to an Agrement formerly entered Into, by this Government and that of St. Augustine to return Mutually all Slaves which should desert From either Province, but on this Occasion it was Refused, the present Governor of St. Augustine acquainting the Deputys that he could not Comply with that Demand, untill His Catholick Majesty should think fit to revoke that Edict.

This

[To the student: use this page to transcribe the text of the document on the opposite page]

Study Questions

1. What does William Bull identify as a main problem facing South Carolina slaveholding society?
2. How did South Carolina and other authorities react to slaves' efforts to reach Spanish Florida? What does that reaction tells us about tensions within southern colonial society and what does it tell about the axes of cooperation?
3. Speculate on the causes of the changing relationship between South Carolina, British authority, and the Spanish. What does the document suggest about the nature and scope of those changes?

Further Reading

Carney, Judith 2002: *Black Rice: The African Origins of Rice Cultivation in the Americas.* Cambridge, MA: Harvard University Press.

Coclanis, Peter A. 1989: *The Shadow of A Dream: Economic Life and Death in the South Carolina Low Country, 1670–1920.* New York: Oxford University Press.

Edgar, Walter 1998: *South Carolina: A History.* Columbia, SC: University of South Carolina Press.

Landers, Jane 1990. Gracia Real de Santa Teresa de Mose: A Free Black Town in Spanish Colonial Florida. 95 *American Historical Review,* 9–30.

Olwell, Robert 1998: *Masters, Slaves, and Subjects: The Culture of Power in the South Carolina Low Country, 1740–1790.* Ithaca, NY: Cornell University Press.

Smith, Mark M. 2005: *Stono: Documenting and Interpreting a Southern Slave Revolt.* Columbia, SC: University of South Carolina Press.

TePaske, John J. 1975: The Fugitive Slave: Intercolonial Rivalry and Spanish Slave Policy, 1687–1764. In Samuel Proctor, ed., *Eighteenth-Century Florida and its Borderlands.* Gainesville, FL: University Press of Florida, 1–12.

Weir, Robert M. 1983: *Colonial South Carolina: A History.* New York: KTO Press.

Wood, Peter H. 1974: *Black Majority: Negroes in Colonial South Carolina from 1670 through the Stono Rebellion.* New York: Alfred Knopf.

Chapter 6

Social Order in the Eighteenth-century South: Slavery and Virginia's Gentry in the 1720s

Context

How to create and preserve order? This question was common to all authorities in colonial America but it took on particular salience in those societies that embraced slavery as the basis of their emerging social and economic system.

By the early eighteenth century Virginia especially was moving into the golden age of the "gentry." The gentry – extremely wealthy, politically powerful elites – were found everywhere in colonial America but their presence was pronounced in the southern colonies, particularly in Virginia and South Carolina. Hallmarks of the gentry usually included involvement and influence in colonial politics, owning large plantations with scores of bondpeople, and a particular cultural "style." This style was reflected in many ways – they read Latin and Greek, for example – but was perhaps most discernable in the gentry's architecture. They embraced classical styles, reminiscent of the English elite and they styled their plantations like English estates. They were anglicized and good enough at emulating the English to convince some aristocratic English travelers that they had achieved the ideal. Witness the travel account of William Huge Grove, an English gentleman, who came to Virginia in 1732:

> I went by ship up the York river, which has pleasant seats on the bank which shew like little villages, for having kitchens, dairy houses, barns, stables, store houses, and some 2 or 3 negro quarters all separate from one another but near the mansion houses. ... the north side is thick seated with gentry on its

> banks with in a mile or at most two from each other ... most of these have pleasant gardens and the prospect of the river render them very pleasant and equal to the Thames from London to Richmond ...

While Virginia's tobacco plantations were not as large as South Carolina's (rice demanded extensive workforces), there were several significant planters with not inconsequential numbers of slaves during the eighteenth century. In the 1720s, for example, 13 percent of slaves in Virginia lived on plantations with 21 or more slaves, with some of the largest of the gentry's plantations holding many more bondpeople.

The gentry's worldview, courtesy of their influence in civic and political affairs, resonated in public architecture too. For example, Virginia's capitol at Williamsburg – construction of "the Palace," as it was called, began in 1706 and finished in 1720 – reflected classical concern as well as contemporary preoccupations with stability, balance, and order. The seat of government and power, it was a highly symmetrical building, balanced and proportioned, and designed to fix order on the land and those who saw it.

The most pronounced expressions of order and power were found on the large plantations. Slave cabins were often arranged down from the Big House, the planter's residence, and constituted small dependencies near enough for labor to be used but far enough away to establish social distance. These plantations were dedicated not simply to economic production but also reflected hierarchy and social authority, an authority increasingly demarcated along racial lines. On Virginia plantations in the early seventeenth century we see the beginnings of the nineteenth-century's powerful planter class, the origins of what has been termed not simply a society with slaves but a full-blown slave society in which bondage underpinned not just the economic workings of the region but inflected the very cultural identity of the increasingly self-aware planter class. This early planter class was close-knit, often united, and conscious – and protective – of its status. It assumed that they were the leaders and custodians of their society and encouraged a deferential attitude among not only blacks but also working and middling whites. By 1750, white Virginians owned about 120,000 slaves, roughly 40 percent of the colony's population.

Virginia did not become a slave society all at once, of course, as the evidence presented in Chapter 2 suggests. Initially, blacks in Virginia enjoyed a degree of freedom. The experience of Anthony Johnson is instructive in this regard. He was sold to the English at Jamestown in 1621 as "Antonio a Negro" and then labored on a plantation for a family called the Bennetts where he proved himself diligent and loyal. The Bennetts favored him and allowed him to farm independently, marry, and baptize his children while still a slave. Eventually, he and his family gained their freedom. Once free, "Antonio" anglicized his name to Anthony Johnson and in 1651 he earned 250 acres of land for sponsoring the entry of servants into the colony. He then bought slaves and began to enter the ranks of the small slaveholding class, growing tobacco and selling it.

After about 1700, however, examples of Anthony Johnson would become fewer as racial slavery solidified in the Chesapeake and Virginia. Antonio Johnson was a member of what has been termed the "Charter Generation" which appeared in North America from the late sixteenth century to about 1680. Cultural creoles, they had encountered European and English society not just in West Africa but also via the West Indies. To some whites, they appeared less alien and were able to adapt culturally and carve out spaces of freedom.

The Charter Generation was followed by the "Plantation Generation" – enslaved people brought across the Atlantic in overwhelming numbers between 1680 and the time of the American Revolution. Less able to integrate into North American society, the Plantation Generation became more insular and used the geographic space of the plantation to recreate African customs and culture. Where profitable staples were grown – tobacco in Virginia and rice in South Carolina – the Plantation Generation took hold and inaugurated the shift from a society with slaves to slave societies where large numbers of enslaved blacks labored on tightly controlled plantations.

The extract of the document presented here allows us to see Virginia's slave society at work on a plantation owned by a member of one of the colony's most influential families – the Randolphs. It also details their relations with neighboring planter families (it appears to have been a member of the Lee family) and illustrates how they attempted to keep control over slaves. The author of the letter is probably William Randolph

(1681–1741) of "Turkey Island," Henrico County, son of the influential William Randolph, patriarch of one of Virginia's leading families. William Randolph the elder was one of the founders of the College of William and Mary and he presided over a family that married into some illustrious lines including the Lee family (from whom General Robert E. Lee was descended) as well as the families of Thomas Jefferson and John Marshall, the influential Supreme Court Justice. This letter suggests the intimacy between two important planter families and explains the ways in which slave labor was used and controlled.

Source

William Randolph [Jr.] to [?], 1722, Custis-Lee Family Papers, Box 1, Richard Bland Lee Papers, 1700–1825, Manuscript Division, Library of Congress, Washington, DC.

Yours by your man Peter I receivd on the 24th but the things your
wife writ for, and one of the Negros being at Jordans, could not Send the People before
this day, Sus goes with them but with much unwillingness, but to incourage her I have
promisd that you'l pass by the Slip She gave you, when you went from our house, and that
if She behaves her Self well, you'l let her come and See her old Father and mother
who are very fond of her. The Silver you Sent for, I have deliverd to Peter an Acco.t
of which at first cost is under mentiond. I have also inclosd a Set of exchange for
£45:1:7½ in part of the money due for your wifes fortune, the receit whereof I desire
youl Signify to me by the first opportunity. My wife and I give our humble
Service to Mr. Lee & his Lady and to your Self and wife. I am

[To the student: use this page to transcribe the text of the document on the opposite page]

Study Questions

1. To what extent and in what ways did William Randolph's slaves enjoy a degree of freedom?
2. What methods did Randolph use to ensure that his slaves did not exploit the latitude he gave them? What mechanisms of control are apparent from the letter?
3. What sorts of connections linked Randolph and the recipient of the letter? How were social ties cemented between members of the gentry?

Further Reading

Bailyn, Bernard 1959: Politics and Social Structure in Virginia. In James Morton Smith, ed., *Seventeenth-Century America: Essays in Colonial History.* Chapel Hill, NC: University of North Carolina Press.

Berlin, Ira 1998: *Many Thousands Gone: The First Two Centuries of Slavery in North America.* Cambridge, MA: Harvard University Press.

Clemens, Paul G. E. 1975: The Operation of an Eighteenth-century Chesapeake Tobacco Plantation. 49 *Agricultural History,* 517–31.

Isaac, Rhys 1982: *The Transformation of Virginia 1740–1790.* New York: W. W. Norton.

Kulikoff, Allan 1986: *Tobacco and Slaves: The Development of Southern Cultures in the Chesapeake, 1680–1800.* Chapel Hill, NC: University of North Carolina Press.

Morgan, Edmund S. 1975: *American Slavery, American Freedom: The Ordeal of Colonial Virginia.* New York: W. W. Norton.

Tate, Thad W. and David L. Ammerman, eds. 1979: *The Chesapeake in the Seventeenth Century: Essays on Anglo-American Society and Politics.* Chapel Hill, NC: University of North Carolina Press.

Walsh, Lorena S. 1993: Slave Life, Slave Society, and Tobacco Production in the Tidewater Chesapeake, 1620–1820. In Ira Berlin and Philip D. Morgan, eds., *Cultivation and Culture: Labor and the Shaping of Slave Life in the Americas.* Charlottesville, VA: University Press of Virginia, 170–99.

Wells, Camille 1993: The Planter's Prospect: Houses, Outbuildings, and Rural Landscapes in Eighteenth-century Virginia. 28 *Winterthur Portfolio,* 1–31.

Chapter 7

The Great Awakening: A Letter to George Whitefield, 1746

Context

In his 1687 theory of gravity, Sir Isaac Newton gave voice to an intellectual idea that would shape colonial America – indeed, the world – in profound ways. By arguing that the universe and everything in it was governed by natural laws which in turn could be understood and explained through human reason, Newton and other seventeenth-century thinkers and scientists articulated the idea of the Enlightenment. Mechanical laws, they claimed, governed everything from the movement of the planters to economics, politics, and human relations. The idea quickly permeated the social realm where Enlightenment thinkers located an important way to rid society of its ills. Apply Reason, they contended, and society will improve.

The idea of natural law was not necessarily at odds with Christian theology. After all, Christianity embraced the idea of natural law and it was perfectly possible for the work of Newton and others to be interpreted as revealing God's glory. Moreover, both the Enlightenment and Protestant Christianity placed a value on literacy and education. That much said, some Americans often welcomed Enlightenment thinking because religion had lost some of its attraction and was perceived as contrary to reason, intellectual and scientific curiosity, and experimentation. Emphasis was placed on observation and verification and the use of microscopes and telescopes especially were popular for verifying and establishing "truth" and adding, literally and metaphorically, perspective on the world. The Enlightenment attracted people interested in the world around them. Benjamin Franklin was a good example. He was a keen inventor, publisher of *Poor Richard's*

Almanac, and an ardent supporter of the generation and preservation of knowledge.

But Enlightenment ideas did not come easily to most Americans and for some they were associated with an excessive secularism and a loss of piety. The clergy especially were worried. To what extent would Deism and skepticism, ways of thinking among educated elites, take hold in the broader population? Would there be a general falling away from godliness? And what of the sprawling colonial frontier? Were settlers' spiritual needs being met? If not, would they retreat into heathenism? Many of these concerns were voiced by the brilliant Congregationalist minister, Jonathan Edwards. In 1726, Edwards assumed charge of a church in Northampton, Massachusetts, and found his congregation despondent, preoccupied with worldly rather than spiritual matters. By the 1730s these worries and concerns gained wide currency and helped give rise to America's first mass movement: The Great Awakening, a huge evangelical movement promising to reinvigorate godliness and Christian piety.

Edwards was important for helping frame the evangelical impulse of the Great Awakening. Touch hearts rather than inform minds, was Edwards' essential credo, even if that meant frightening people toward God and rejuvenating faith by stressing the perils of hell. Arguably even more important for animating and spreading the "awakening" was the English Wesleyan minister, George Whitefield, whose calls for individual salvation and the need for ministers to inspire fervor in their congregations had taken England by storm. Whitefield arrived in the colonies to spread his message in 1739 and preached to huge crowds. Whitefield's message was powerful and delivered with passion, so much so that even those inclined toward Enlightenment thinking, including Benjamin Franklin, found Whitefield's call persuasive. Whitefield's mass meetings were highly charged affairs. People wept and shouted and vocally proclaimed their need for salvation.

Imitators of Whitefield were not slow to follow and by the 1740s the colonies were gripped with the evangelical spirit. The message resonated with all levels of colonial society. Slaves, laborers, elites, women, seamen, all found the emotional component of the Great Awakening compelling, authentic, and rewarding. Between 1740 and 1742, for example, up to 50,000 people – educated and unchurched alike – joined churches in New England alone and revivalism was just as, and perhaps more, popular on the frontier and in the southern colonies.

Only the more traditional clergy remained unimpressed by what they perceived as a revolutionary and irresponsible theology, replete with writhing bodies, excessive noise, and undisciplined behavior. It was the devil's work, some claimed, pointing to the sometimes manic behavior of those who converted. They also criticized the self-proclaimed ministers leading the revivals, especially on the frontier, as uneducated. Many of them, including slaves and the working poor, were indeed unschooled, their power residing in their message and their ability to deliver rousing sermons. Traditional ministers also argued that revivalism was dangerous to social order and the democratic aspect of the Great Awakening worried them tremendously.

As revivalism played itself out, Enlightenment concerns with rationality began to percolate the Great Awakening, adding a calmer quality to the movement. While Enlightenment thinkers and clergy agreed that revivalism had exposed the failings of traditional Christianity, especially the strictures of orthodox Calvinism, they refused to import in its entirety the emotionalism of the revivals. Instead, they used the idea of natural law, of rationality, and combined it with a newly awakened sense of responsibility for the spiritual well-being of their congregations. Moreover, many itinerant preachers and unschooled ministers who had spearheaded the Great Awakening began to become better educated in the finer points of doctrine and theology, partly in reaction to the traditionalists' critique of their unschooled methods. In the end, the Great Awakening and the Enlightenment braided, both serving to inspire faith in American and human progress and both calling into question the sanctity of unquestioned tradition. In some ways, both movements helped foster nascent ideas about the desirability of breaking with the past and embracing a different future. Such ideas, in the context of the mid-eighteenth century, were potentially revolutionary.

The excerpt offered here is from the pen – the at times very cramped pen – of Susanna Bayard of the Eastern Shore of Maryland. Samuel Bayard, who likely built Great House in 1717–20, died in 1721 and left it to Susanna, where she lived until her passing in 1750. Susanna Bayard was a highly educated woman and spoke and wrote French, Latin, English, and Dutch. Deeply pious, she evidently thought a great deal about theology and salvation and her letter to George Whitefield – one of several – clearly shows a fine mind at work. She was a close friend of Whitefield, who noted his affection for her in his diary. He was a frequent correspondent with Susanna Bayard and had stayed with her at Great House several times, beginning in 1740 (he even had the northwest bedchamber named after him – "Whitefield's Room").

Source

Susanna Bayard to George Whitefield, Bohemia, Maryland, 10 July 1746, Manuscript Division, Library of Congress, Washington, DC.

11 Maryland Bohemia River 10 July 1746

Revd & very honoured

Sir

I Receivd Your very Agreable favour Dated June ye 30th with thankfulness & a lively feeling of My vileness & utter
Unworthiness which Makes Me wonder that I should Employ Your thoughts one
Moment Dear Sr You Could Not wish Me a More Glorious Peacefull & Securer Place then
at My Dear Lord Jesus feet I do Begg importunately His Divine Majesty that there May be
the Place of My Abode while I Live O the Blessed feet of My Lord No tongue Can Express what Comfort the
Broken hearted humble Sinners finds there in al My temptations Afflictions & Tribulations
I have Not found a Remedy More Efficatious then the Remembrance of the wounds & Merits
of My Exceeding Precious Redeemer My Lord He Died for Me what Made of His Precious Blood
And Glorious Prayers An infinite treasure of Satisffaction & Merits So that I find in that Precious
Blood of My Dear Lord A Balsem Sufficient to Cure all the wounds of My Poor Soul & fountain to
wash away al the Scarlate and Crimson Dye My Soul has Been Polluted with by Sin It Gives
Me a full Assurance trough All My Doubts & fears Becaus All My hopes is fixed in the Death
And Resurrection of My Triomphant Lord and May it Please His Divine Majesty to fill My h[eart]
and Soul with an humble Confidence in his Merits Since by faith he has Given Me to fly
to Him in All occasions as to the Citty of Refuge there I do Desier to Live and Die the Love
that I find in My Dear Lord Jesus for vile And wretched Me And the Love which by faith
He has kindeled in My Soul for Him will Bannish More and More from My heart All fears
And Doublings Arising from that Cursed Principle of Unbelief which I am Persuaded the He
Can Deliver Me from whom He thinks fitt tho I have Served My Lord But very Poorly I Must
Say So with Deep Mourning and humiliation Before Him Yet I Can Say with afflicted Peter
Lord thou knowest all things thou knowest that I Love thee My Soul Desiers to
Begin again in great Earnest to Give My Self in Love to My Lord in all Manner of
Holy obedience And Self Denial May My Life hence forth Be hidden with Christ in God

[To the student: use this page to transcribe the text of the document on the opposite page]

Study Questions

1. What was Susanna Bayard's view of God and His relationship with the individual?
2. What is the tone of the letter? Is it theologically inclined or does it have an emotional, revivalist component to it?
3. Speculate on what George Whitefield might have said in reply to Susanna Bayard's letter.

Further Reading

Bercovitch, S. 1986: *The American Jeremiad*. Madison, WI: University of Wisconsin Press.

Bonomi, Patricia U. 1986: *Under the Cope of Heaven: Religion, Society, and Politics in Colonial America*. New York: Oxford University Press.

Butler, Jon 1982. Enthusiasm Described and Decried: The Great Awakening as Interpretive Fiction. *Journal of American History* 69, 305–25.

Gaustad, Edwin S. 1957: *The Great Awakening in New England*. New York: Harper.

Hatch, Nathan 1989: *The Democratization of American Christianity.* New Haven: Yale University Press.

Heimert, A. 1966: *Religion and the American Mind: From the Great Awakening to the Revolution*. Cambridge, MA: Harvard University Press.

Isaac, Rhys 1974: Evangelical Revolt: The Nature of the Baptists' Challenge to the Tradition Order in Virginia, 1765–1775. *William and Mary Quarterly* 3rd series, 31, 345–68.

Lambert, Frank 1994: *Pedlar in Divinity: George Whitefield and the Transatlantic Revivals, 1737–1770*. Princeton, NJ: Princeton University Press.

May, Henry F. 1976: *The Enlightenment in America*. New York: Oxford University Press.

Woolverton, J. F. 1984: *Colonial Anglicanism in North America*. Detroit: Wayne State University Press.

Chapter 8

Empire and Native Americans: The Treaty of Lancaster, 1744

Context

Central to British imperial design at mid-century was the idea of consolidation, the physical securing of space and empire. Negotiating with Native Americans was critical to such efforts not least because Indian nations, though sometimes weakened by colonization, retained sufficient power and influence to require some accommodation and diplomacy on the part of the British.

That the British needed to negotiate with some key Native American groups suggests just how important the Indian presence was to colonial life, not just in the earliest years of "settlement" but throughout the entire period and, in fact, beyond. Colonists traded, mixed, and fought with Native Americans and their presence cannot and should not be discounted. That much said, what are we to make of this presence? How best to characterize it?

Here, it is worth pausing to consider a number of competing interpretations offered by various historians concerning the most accurate way to understand the nature of Indian-settler relations. According to Francis Jennings' pioneering 1975 study, *The Invasion of America*, Europeans were ruthless in conquest not of "virgin" land but of "widowed" land. The "savages" in his telling were the Europeans who used extraordinary force and violence to wrest land and property from Indians, whose diplomacy was cheap and vicious, and who made no apology for their dedicated destruction of Indian culture and society. From this perspective, any treaties signed by Indian nations with European powers were largely coerced, always one-sided, and put the Indian at a distinct disadvantage. Conversely, Richard White's more recent work, *The Middle Ground* (1991), argues that Indians of the upper Great Lakes especially managed to work in a geographical and metaphoric "middle ground" with European powers, forcing colonial authorities to negotiate and sometimes acquiesce to their demands. White characterizes Imperial-Indian relations as more plastic, with a good deal of give-and-take, a world in which Native Americans used their skills, intelligence, and cultural flexibility to navigate the treacherous shoals of British and French imperialism in an effort to preserve some of their authority and even flourish in certain quarters. Debate among historians is so pronounced not least because a good deal of Indian history – what the Indians themselves thought and their value systems – remains hard to fathom and document. Even the best documented nation, the Iroquois, remain elusive.

The Treaty of Lancaster, signed in 1744, and presented in part here, reflected not only the British policy of imperial consolidation but hints at just how important colonial-Indian relations were to heightening tension and, in the long term, the coming of the American Revolution. Claiming to speak for a number of mid-Atlantic Indian nations, the Iroquois were instrumental in negotiating the treaty. Essentially, the terms of the treaty pushed the Iroquois and several Indian nations west of the Alleghenies so that colonists might expand westward. It was hardly the only important treaty of the period and should be read in the context of a fairly deep genealogy of arrangements that British authorities made with a variety of Native American groups. Virginia's 1677 Treaty of Middle Plantation, for example, defined reservations for the Pamunkey and Mattoponi and required them to pay an annual quitrent measured in beaver skins. Other treaties either limited British settlement or empowered one Indian nation at the expense of another. In Virginia alone, the Albany Treaty of 1684 limited English settlement in areas of Virginia's Piedmont while the Albany Conference allowed the Iroquois to hunt on Manahoac lands and circumscribed the geography of Algonquian tribes. But the Treaty of Lancaster was especially damaging to Native Americans of the region and particularly revealing of British imperial policy. It was also critical in helping bring about, if even indirectly, conflict between Britain and France a decade later, a conflict that, eventually, led to the unraveling of Britain's North American Empire.

The French-Indian War, also called the Seven Years' War, 1756–63 (the war lasted actually nine years, 1754–63, but it was formally seven years because Britain did not make a declaration of war until 1756) reveals Native Americans as victims of imperial policy and as actors in it. This war was part of a much larger contest between Britain and France in Europe and it bled into the colonies and involved Native Americans to a considerable extent.

The war started in 1754 when a number of Virginians, doubtless flush with expansionist impulses courtesy of the Treaty of Lancaster, crossed over the Appalachians into the Upper Ohio Valley to trade with Indians and to survey 200,000 acres of land which had been granted to them by King George. From the Virginians' perspective, treaties such as those signed at Lancaster gave rise to an expansionist mentality and the push westward into more Indian lands was simply part and parcel of the larger colonial and British project. For years, however, the French had had a foothold in the region, principally as traders with Native Americans, and they perceived these new efforts by English colonists as aggressive and as a threat to their livelihood. The area quickly fell into dispute and the French began building a number of forts to secure and defend their claim to the region.

Britain responded in 1755 by sending George Washington and Major General Edward Braddock to halt French expansion. Their efforts failed and they were forced to retreat to Virginia. A year later, John Campbell, the Earl of Loudoun, took command of the British forces in North America. He was not an effective commander and the British continued to lose to the French not least because the French managed to ally themselves with disgruntled and politically savvy Indian groups in the region.

In the long run, though, British military power prevailed and as they won more victories, Native Americans, again anticipating what the future might look like, began to shift their allegiance to the British from the French, a realignment that in itself helped British forces finally prevail in the Canadian and American colonies. The British won the French-Indian War and in 1763 signed the Treaty of Paris, the terms of which were critical for consolidating British control of North America. The treaty essentially ended the French presence on the North American continent and established Britain as the preeminent colonial power.

Yet victory sowed the seeds of destruction. The war had been expensive and the British, having now secured much of the continent, were obliged to centralize their gains and prevent France from recapturing it. To this end, Britain kept a significant military force stationed in the colonies. As English settlers began to swarm farther westward, tensions with Native Americans increased and demanded even greater military involvement on the part of the British. In 1763 Pontiac, an Ottawa chief, organized several interior tribes and began to resist the British, capturing all the British outposts west of Pittsburgh. It took yet more military intervention to smother the rebellion. Britain's national debt had doubled after 1754 and supporting the troops in colonial America added to the financial drain.

To offset the cost, George Grenville, the First Lord of the Treasury began to institute a series of measures, many of which targeted colonial Americans directly. In 1764, for example, the British passed the Revenue Act (also known as the Sugar Act) in an effort to enforce and increase the amount of tax colonial merchants paid the British government. A slew of other measures – the Currency Act of 1764, the Quartering Act of 1765, and, most famously, the Stamp Act of 1765, among others – were all designed to make colonial Americans pay for the military cost of fighting the Seven Years' War and for the continuing presence of the British army on the continent. As we will see, such measures, in combination with other factors, heightened tensions between mother country and colonists in the 1760s and helped map out the beginnings of American resistance to British rule. For the moment, though, it is important to remember the central role Native Americans played in British imperial schemes, how they influenced events, and how very embedded they were in questions concerning expansion, imperial design, and war during the key decades leading up to the Revolution.

Source

The Treaty of Lancaster, 25 October 1744, The Ethel Ames Collection of Lee Family Papers, Box 2, Family Correspondence, Thomas Lee, 1720–1750, Manuscript Division, Library of Congress, Washington, DC.

To all People to whom these presents shall come: Canasateego Tachanoontia Jonuhat Caxhayion Torachdadon Neecokanyhak & Rocirrawuchto Sachems or chiefs of the nation of the Onondagons, Taguchsoonyunt Gachraddedow, Hucasaly-akon, Rowanhohiso, Osochquah, Seayenties Sachems or chiefs of the nation of the Cahugas, Swadany alias Shickelimy Onichuaaqua, Onoch-Kally drury alias Watathua, Tohashwan=rorow, Aroghochthaw, and Tior-Haasery Sachems or chiefs of the nation of the Tuscaroras, Tanasanegos, and Tanichiuntus Sachems or chiefs of the nation of the Senikers send greeting Whereas the six United Nations of Indians laying claim to some lands in the Colony of Virginia signified their willingness to enter into a treaty concerning the same. Whereupon Thomas Lee esqr. a member in ordinary of his Majesty's honourable council of State and one of the Judges of the supreme court of judicature in that Colony, and William Beverly esqr. colonel and county lieut. of the county of Orange and one of the representatives of the people in the house of Burgesses of that colony, were deputed by the governor of the said colony, as commissioners to treat with the said six nations or their deputies, Sachems or chiefs as well of and concerning the said claim, as to renew their covenant chain between the said colony & the said six nations and the said commissionrs. having met at Lancaster in Lancaster county, and province of Pensylvania, and as a foundation for a stricter amity and peace at this juncture agreed with the said Sachems or chiefs of the said six nations for a disclaimer and renunciation of all their claim or pretence of right whatsoever of the said six nations, and an acknowledgment of the right of our sovereign the King of Great Britain to all the land in the said Colony of Virginia. Now Know ye that for and in consideration of the sum of four hundred pounds current money of Pensylvania paid and delivered to the above named Sachems or chiefs partly in goods and partly in Gold money by the said commissioners, they the said sachems or chiefs on behalf of the said six nations do hereby renounce and disclaim not only all the right of the said six nations, but also recognize and acknowledge the right and title of our sovereign the King of Great Britain to all the lands within the said colony as it is now or hereafter may be peopled and bounded by his said Majesty our sovereign Lord the

[To the student: use this page to transcribe the text of the document on the opposite page]

Study Questions

1. With whom were the British dealing and what were the expressed terms of the treaty?
2. Is it possible to use this source to say anything about Native Americans themselves or is the source revealing only of British policy and attitudes?
3. What is the tone of the treaty? Does it suggest anything about the deeper cultural attitudes of colonial British America toward Native Americans?

Further Reading

Andersen, Fred 2001: *Crucible of War: The Seven Years' War and the Fate of Empire in British North America, 1754–1766*. New York: Vintage.

Axtell, James 1981: *The European and the Indian: Essays in the Ethnohistory of Colonial North America*. New York: Oxford University Press.

Axtell, James 1985: *The Invasion Within: The Contest of Cultures in Colonial North America*. New York: Oxford University Press.

Cayton, Andrew R. L. and Fredrika J. Teute, eds. *Contact Points: American Frontiers from the Mohawk Valley to the Mississippi, 1750–1830*. Chapel Hill, NC: University of North Carolina Press.

Jennings, Francis 1975: *The Invasion of America: Indians, Colonialism, and the Cant of Conquest*. Chapel Hill, NC: University of North Carolina Press.

Jennings, Francis 1990: *The Empire of Fortune: Crowns, Colonies and Tribes in the Seven Years War in America*. New York: W. W. Norton.

Richter, Daniel K. 1992: *The Ordeal of the Longhouse: The Peoples of the Iroquois League in the Era of Colonization*. Chapel Hill, NC: University of North Carolina Press.

Usner, Daniel H. Jr. 1992: *Indians, Settlers, and Slaves in a Frontier Exchange Economy: The Lower Mississippi Valley before 1783*. Chapel Hill, NC: University of North Carolina Press.

White, Richard 1991: *The Middle Ground: Indians, Empires, and Republics in the Great Lakes Region, 1650–1815*. New York: Cambridge University Press.

Chapter 9

Imperial Crises and the Coming of Revolution: The Politicization of a Colonial Merchant, 1765

Context

In the mid-eighteenth century, most colonial Americans, at least those with an English background, tended to pride themselves on being, well, "English." Lots of towns and places derived their names from England, colonies tended to model themselves politically after the English model, many colonists consumed English goods, and there was a general admiration for the system of English civil liberties.

Important differences were evolving, however – differences that tended to set the English apart from the colonists. In terms of economics, England tended increasingly to be influenced by large scale corporations. The Bank of England ran much of the Empire's finances, industry was beginning to become factory-based, and agriculture was run by gentry who owned large estates and who hired men and women to perform agricultural labor. By contrast, there was comparatively little manufacturing in the colonies, a higher proportion of colonists (compared to their English counterparts) owned their own land, most farmsteads were small and modest (with the exception of southern plantations), and it was a much less urban and more rural society than England. For example, in 1790 London was a teeming colossus of 675,000 while 90 percent of all colonists lived in towns of fewer than 2,000 people.

Economic inequality also marked difference between colony and mother country. England experienced very deep class divisions and the elite enjoyed a system of inherited privileges. Members of eighteenth-century England's upper class constituted less than 2 percent of the country's population but owned 70 percent of its land. Also, by right of birth, English aristocrats claimed membership in the House of Lords and the House of Commons was not made up of commoners but, rather, dominated by powerful families. While prominent families certainly held great sway in the colonies, they were generally a pale reflection of their English counterparts. Yes, some families were extremely influential economically, culturally, and politically but there was no titled ruling class holding political privilege by hereditary right in the colonies. Moreover, wealth was spread more evenly in colonial America. England's lower classes were larger and worse off than those in the colonies; less than a third of England's inhabitants belonged to the "middling sort" of traders, professionals, artisans, farmers; more than two-thirds struggled for survival at the bottom of society. By contrast, the colonial middle class counted for nearly three-quarters of the white population.
In colonial America, land was cheaper, labor was scarcer, wages were higher, and it was easier for

white colonials to save money and buy a farm of their own.

Even though they admired the English political system, colonials were also becoming increasingly ambivalent about its actual functioning. They were especially critical of what they perceived as rank corruption with the placement of the monarch's ministers in key political positions. Patronage, they claimed, had undermined the virtues of the English system of government and had percolated all levels of the political system. Colonial Americans liked to think that their colonial governments mirrored the ideal English one but did not suffer from its corruption. In fact, colonial America was less susceptible to patronage and electoral manipulation. Royal governors, for example, had less patronage power while colonial assemblies had more since only they could levy taxes. Moreover, even if governors had more authority they were less able to use it since almost 70 percent of all white adult colonial men were enfranchised. Property requirements for voting were often the same as they were in England but widespread ownership of land allowed most white men to meet the qualifications.

Although the problem of patronage was to become important in generating tension between the colonies and Britain during and after the 1760s, prior to about 1760 the matter had little popular purchase. In fact, many colonial Americans were relatively free from the influence of the mother country. Economic policies, particularly mercantilist ones regulating trade between England and the colonies, rested lightly on the shoulders of most colonial Americans. Britain pursued what has been termed a policy of "benign neglect" in the colonies. Colonials, in fact, seemed to enjoy the relationship. Britain appeared distant and many felt that they could be better Englishmen in colonial America than they could in England.

The cost of the Seven Year's War and the decision by the British government to shift some of the financial responsibility to the colonies to help repay the debt and support the military presence on the continent was an important factor in beginning a process whereby colonial Americans became increasingly alienated from the mother country. Because colonial Americans believed that property guaranteed liberty and that they should always remain suspicious of concentrations of political power, they came to view British efforts to tax them, without their consent, as an attack on their freedom by a corrupt political system. This intellectual association between property, power, and liberty was critical in informing colonial reaction to the various measures proposed and enforced by Lord Grenville, First Lord of the Treasury, and Chancellor of the Exchequer. For example, they perceived the Sugar Act and the Stamp Act as illegitimate and dangerous because both were taxes passed by members of Parliament in London, none of whom had been elected by colonials in America.

There were also important economic implications associated with all of Grenville's measures. The Sugar or Revenue Act passed on April 5, 1764, for example, was a revised version of the 1733 Sugar and Molasses Act, which required colonial merchants to pay a tax of six pence per gallon on the importation of foreign molasses. Colonial merchants, though, largely avoided paying the tax, used French sources instead, and so decreased English revenue, damaging in particular the British West Indies market. Grenville's 1764 Sugar Act in fact reduced the rate of tax on molasses from six pence to three pence per gallon but provided for a much more robust enforcement of the Act. It was this enforcement, backed by the British navy, which caused a steep decline in the colonial production of rum, the effect of which was to reduce the colonial trade with the French West Indies and elsewhere, markets that were also important for colonial exports of cheese, flour, and lumber. In effect, the Sugar Act of 1764 hit the middle and New England colonies especially hard, particularly its merchants, reducing the amount of currency they could generate and limiting their ability to buy British manufactured goods.

The Stamp Act, passed the following year, was more directly an effort by Grenville to raise revenue from the colonies. It taxed virtually all legal documents, newspapers, contracts, pamphlets, and playing cards in the colonies. For many American colonists, though, the taxes were not simply an economic question. They were understood as squarely political. Grenville's measures seem to confirm the long held suspicion in the colonies that corrupt English officials were conspiring against American liberties.

As a result of the Sugar, Stamp, and a series of other acts, colonists protested. During the spring and summer of 1765 American colonial assemblies passed resolves denying that Parliament had the authority to pass taxes – they argued that the right to tax Americans belonged to colonial assemblies alone. Virginia took the lead in 1765 and passed the Virginia Resolves, stating that it was Virginia's exclusive right to tax Virginians. This, in turn, prompted several colonies to pass new resolves calling for the repeal of the Stamp and Sugar Acts, inspired groups of merchants to agree to stop importing English goods, and led to the emergence of a new resistance group that styled themselves the "Sons of Liberty" which protested the new measures, sometimes violently. For a number of reasons, Parliament repealed the Stamp Act in March 1766.

The matter did not end there and tensions increased between Britain and the colonies during the 1760s. Although the specifics changed – for example, Charles Townshend, the new Chancellor of the Exchequer, instigated a number of new acts, taxes, and disciplinary measures – and while mounting tensions took new, particular forms – such as the Boston Massacre of 1770 – the basic tensions expressed over the Sugar and Stamp Acts remained key to understanding the economic and political nature of the dispute between Parliament and American colonists. The War for Independence was not set in stone, of course, but because property and liberty were so tightly braided in colonial minds efforts by the British to institute taxes, especially if there was a hint or suspicion of corruption, were very likely to generate complaints and spark some potentially revolutionary sentiments.

The following two notes, both from John Lownes, a Philadelphia merchant, to William Freeman, a merchant in Bristol, England, suggest how politics quickly entered the mindset of the commercial class. In the first letter, written in late July 1765, Lownes places a typical order with Freeman for some cheese and instructs him on amount, price, and care of the commodity. His second note is terse and is written some four months after his first, by which time news of the Stamp Act had made it to colonial America.

Source

John Lownes, Philadelphia, to William Freeman, Bristol, entries for July 29, November 19, 1765, John Lownes Letterbook, 1760–1769, Manuscript Division, Library of Congress, Washington, DC.

Philada July 29. 1765

Estemed Friend

I would have Thee send mee by first opertunity After these comes to hand one thousand weight lb of good Sound gloster Chees to weigh from 14 to 18 lb pr Chees allso five hundred weight of Chees to weigh between 20 & 30 lb pr Chees by Every opertunity to this port for one 12 Monthes Except for bid & If the Capt that brings them will stow them in an Arrey plase in the Cabin or Sterige & Delever them in good order I will allow him one Doller on 15 hundred Weight besides his primige Remaine with respect thy friend

John Lowne

P. S besure that they be Not bought packed or Shiped till the Vesel is Nigh Saling & Insure as soone as they becomes my property

To

William Freeman

Mt in Bristol

[To the student: use this page to transcribe the text of the document on the opposite page]

Philad.a ~~4~~ Novembr 19 1765

Estemed Friend

I wrote Thee of the 29 of July last ordering som Chees but since that You have Sent us the Unwelcom —

STAMP ACT theirfore pleas to Observe the Contentes of the ~~[illegible]~~ * Inclosed and If wee should be so happey as to have the Act Repeled then Continue as Pr Order of July 29th — — Remaine with Respect

Thy friend John Lownes

To

William Freeman Merts.
In Bristol Pr the Traphany
Capn Smith

[To the student: use this page to transcribe the text of the document on the opposite page]

Study Questions

1. What do we learn about the world of merchants from these documents? What sort of information did they exchange?
2. Suggest why Lownes ordered, of all commodities, cheese.
3. What is Lownes saying to Freeman in the second note? Is he engaging in simply economic activity or is there a political import to what he writes?

Further Reading

Appleby, Joyce 1978: The Social Origins of American Revolutionary Ideology. *Journal of American History* 64, 939–58.

Bailyn, Bernard 1976: *The Ideological Origins of the American Revolution*. Cambridge, MA: Harvard University Press.

Breen, T. H. 1993: Narrative of Commercial Life: Consumption, Ideology, and Community on the Eve of the American Revolution. 50 *William and Mary Quarterly* 3rd series, 471–501.

Egnal, Marc 1988: *A Mighty Empire: The Origins of the American Revolution*. Ithaca, NY: Cornell University Press.

Greene, Jack P. 1986: *Peripheries and Centers: Constitutional Development in the Extended Polities of the British Empire and the United States, 1607–1788*. Athens, GA: University of Georgia Press.

Morgan, Edmund S. and Helen M. Morgan 1963: *The Stamp Act Crisis*. New York: Collier Books.

Nash, Gary B. 1979: *The Urban Crucible: Social Change, Political Consciousness, and the Origins of the American Revolution*. Cambridge, MA: Harvard University Press.

Olton, Charles S. 1975: *Artisans for Independence: Philadelphia Mechanics and the American Revolution*. Syracuse, NY: Syracuse University Press.

Schlesinger, Arthur M. 1968: *The Colonial Merchants and the American Revolution*. New York: Athenaeum.

Chapter 10

Fighting the Revolutionary War:
A Woman on the Homefront, 1776

Context

The actual beginning of the American Revolution did not answer fully several pressing questions: who was an "American," would they fight and, if so, for what, precisely?

We begin in Boston after the Royal Governor of Massachusetts, General Thomas Gage, had dissolved the colony's legislature only to see it and many others reform as provincial congresses. Massachusetts' new provincial congress, learning that Parliament considered the colonies were in a state of rebellion, began arming the militia. In response, Gage started to fortify Boston and was ordered by British commander, Lord North, to seize the leaders of the Provincial Congress thus, hoped North, beheading the rebellion. The colonists had guessed that Gage would attempt such a thing and had been surveying the British. When Gage moved out of Boston toward Concord on April 18, 1775, where he aimed to capture the Provincial Congress' supplies, the colonists were prepared. Between the British under Gage and Concord lay Lexington.

The story is among the most famous in American history. When news of the British march to Concord reached Lexington, the town's seventy or so militia men (mostly farmers) mustered on Lexington Green where, in the early morning, they were met with 700 professional British redcoats. The British commander ordered the militia to disburse and, sensibly, they began to do so. No one knows who fired the first shot just after the militia was ordered to leave but we do know that a chain reaction occurred and the British left eight Americans dead at Lexington before they set off for Concord. The British were less successful at Concord. They were so overwhelmed by the hundreds of sharp shooting militia men that they retreated to Boston where they soon found themselves under siege.

The bloodshed at Lexington and Concord in effect committed colonials to rebellion and independence. Such, at least, was the conclusion a man named Thomas Paine drew from these events. Paine was not American – he was British by birth – but quickly became American by attitude and, ironically, helped inspire American nationalism. In 1776 he wrote a pamphlet to inform colonials of their identity as a distinct people and their national destiny. *Common Sense* enjoyed tremendous popularity and wide circulation, selling 120,000 copies within three months of its publication. Paine stirred national thinking by criticizing the entire British system from the perspective of republican ideology. Denouncing monarchy as foolish and dangerous and chastising George III personally, Paine rejected the idea that colonials were or should want to be English and argued that Americans were different. Americans were republicans, not monarchists, and he argued that it was simple "common sense" that Americans wanted to be independent of Britain. Not everyone was persuaded by Paine initially but enough were so that in answer to the question, would Americans fight, increasingly men and women said "yes." But what, exactly, would they fight for? And was there still a chance of reconciliation with Britain?

The delegates to the Second Continental Congress in Philadelphia in May 1775 answered both questions. A month after Lexington and Concord, they met to determine whether independence or reconciliation was the best course. There were a few very strong advocates for complete independence (such as John Adams) but there were also more moderate voices who feared that chaos and social dislocation would result if the colonies pushed too hard or fast for independence. The splits among the delegates gave the deliberations and pronouncements of the Second Continental Congress a schizophrenic flavor. For example, they drew up the Olive Branch Petition in July 1775 affirming American loyalty to George III and asked the king to disavow the actions of his ministers. Yet Congress, in separate action a month earlier, had authorized the creation of a military force – the Continental Army – and had issued paper money to pay for the troops. In response, George III refused to even receive the Olive Branch Petition.

This attitude and the publication of *Common Sense* in 1776 empowered the radicals which, in turn, resulted in the Declaration of Independence stating that Americans no longer considered themselves English and denied Britain any authority in the colonies. Congress adopted it on July 4, 1776.

It is important to note, however, that the sentiment for independence was not universal in 1776. Americans who would not back the rebellion numbered about one-fifth of the population in 1775. They called themselves "Loyalists"; the "rebels" called them Tories – "a thing whose head is in England, whose body is in America, and whose neck ought to be stretched." In truth, the Loyalists were not simple traitors. Some, in fact, had protested against the Stamp Act. But these men and women feared what they perceived as the radicalism of the revolution and worried about the stability of their society without Britain to maintain control.

As despised as they were by Patriots, the Loyalists were too few in number to pose a serious threat to the American cause. The British army was another matter. Highly trained soldiers and experienced officers were the backbone of the army and were a formidable opponent. At the height of the war there were 50,000 British troops augmented by 30,000 Hessian mercenaries from Germany as well as a very significant British naval presence facing the colonists. The Americans were in a slightly different position. Certainly they had good leadership in George Washington. But his Continental Army in 1775 numbered just 16,000, drawn from the militia, and most were not professional soldiers. In fact, this Continental "Regular" army had trouble attracting recruits. Most preferred to fight as members of their local militias – as "irregular" troops – who turned out when the British came near their homes. Washington tried to compensate for this weakness by devising a defensive strategy. He hoped to avoid exposing raw rebel troops on open ground where British discipline and experience would win the day and instead planned to fight the British from strong fortifications.

Much of the war was won on the battlefield, and that story is well known, but we should be careful to remember the importance of the homefront. Civilians had to be supportive of this war if soldiers were to prevail. There is no doubt that many men and women thought carefully about the nature of the war, its meaning, and its prosecution. Equally important was the way in which the British and the Hessians alienated any residual sympathy in the country. Wherever the British were stationed, food shortages resulted and social tensions increased. British troops took housing, sometimes damaged property, and the Hessians further infuriated locals with their brutish behavior, all important factors helping to erode whatever loyalist sympathy some Americans may have had.

Arguably a turning point in the Revolutionary War was France's decision to intervene in the war following a series of American victories in 1777. Although France had secretly been supplying the rebel army since the spring of 1776, there was no formal alliance. The British defeat at Saratoga enabled Benjamin Franklin to arrange a treaty favorable to the Americans with France, signed in 1778. Under the terms, both parties agreed to independence for America. The treaty left the British no choice but to declare war on France and a year later, Spain too, when Spain joined the alliance with France and America. Britain was now overstretched and embroiled in a transatlantic war.

The war raged on for three more years until, at the end of September 1781, Lord Cornwallis found himself sandwiched at Yorktown, Virginia. Behind him loomed the French navy, at his front and to the sides stood 7,800 French soldiers, 5,700 continentals, and 3,200 militia. Cornwallis had fewer men and nowhere to go. He surrendered and the war was over.

We know little about the author of this letter, Margaret Livingston. She wrote it from Fairfield, Connecticut in 1776 to her sister, Catherine Livingston

Ridley, second wife of Maryland merchant, Matthew Ridley. What is apparent, however, is the extent to which this woman was keenly aware of the political developments of and conversations about the war. Her strongly held beliefs and opinions about liberty, its prosecution, and threats to the American cause are readily apparent. More than simply engaging in the boycotting of British goods – a common political act by women generally during the Revolutionary War – the letter excerpted here suggests the extent to which the Revolutionary War percolated the homefront. At a time when women had few legal powers, Margaret Livingston's letter reminds us that women could be fully engaged in political discourse even if that discourse was private and between family members.

Source

Margaret Livingston to [Catherine Livingston], October 20, 1776, Ridley Family Papers II, Massachusetts Historical Society, Boston, Massachusetts.

Your last favor my dear Caty should have been answered long before this, had I not thought I should have had the happiness of seeing you ~~before this~~ I dont yet despair of that pleasure; we are all so very anxious to be in your Province that nothing but the impossibility of going there will hinder us, you no doubt will be surpriz'd at our undertaking such a journey at this season of the Year, the necessaries of Life are so exceeding scarce & high that if we are obliged to stay here, I dont know what will become of us, our present Stock consists of a little Poultry, 2 lb of Butter, & a few pounds of Pork, where we are to get more we dont know, I cant help exclaiming now & then, dreadful fruits of Liberty, I confess I have not such romantic notions of the Goddess that your Ladyship has, you know our Sex are doomed to be obedient in every stage of life so that we shant be great gainers by this contest, tell Cousin Susan I think it is high time the Congress should make the resolve that made us laugh so much, this War must take off a number of Men as they keep dying all the while as my neighbors say, it would distress you to see the poor objects that come home with the Camp difficulty, This Evening a large Ship appeared in sight, which has made the weak nerved among quite low spirited, to be serious, I dont think our habitation the safest in the world, we are but about a Mile & a half from where the Ships can lay, & the Torys they say begin to be very troublesome, they have vowed vengeance against this place, as many of them have been confined in the Goal here, I am [illegible] afraid of them, they are in general the lowest people in the Colony, I wish I was in the Jerseys, Nanny Browne & Suky went last Thursday they had like to have been at the place where the Regulars are, they try'd to get to East Chester the [illegible] night before the Regulars landed how surpriz'd would they have been in the morning to have seen themselves surrounded by them, Suky, all this Summer has been wishing to see

[To the student: use this page to transcribe the text of the document on the opposite page]

Study Questions

1. What is the tone of Margaret Livingston's letter to her sister?
2. Identify the principal political points she makes in the letter.
3. What hardships did the War cause her and her family?

Further Reading

Berkin, Carol 2006: *Revolutionary Mothers: Women in the Struggle for America's Independence*. New York: Vintage.

Calhoon, Robert M. 1976: Civil, Revolutionary, or Partisan: The Loyalists and the Nature of the War for Independence. In Stanley J. Underdahl, ed., *Military History of the American Revolution: The Proceedings of the 6th Military History Symposium United States Air Force Academy 10–11 October 1974*. Washington: Office of Air Force History, 93–108.

Higginbotham, Don 1971: *The War of American Independence: Military Attitudes, Policies, and Practice, 1763–1789*. New York: Macmillan.

Jensen, Merrill 1968: *The Founding of a Nation: A History of the American Revolution, 1763–1776*. New York: Oxford University Press.

Middlekauff, Robert 1982: *The Glorious Cause: The American Revolution 1763–1789*. New York: Oxford University Press.

Raphael, Ray 2002: *A People's History of the American Revolution: How Common People Shaped the Fight for Independence*. New York: Harper Perennial.

Resch, John and Walter Sargent, eds. 2006: *War and Society in the American Revolution: Mobilization and Home Fronts*. Dekalb, IL: Northern Illinois University Press.

Rosswurm, Steven. 1985: The Pursuit of Context: War and Society in the American Revolution. 13 *Reviews in American History*, 242–6.

Royster, Charles W. 1980: *A Revolutionary People at War: The Continental Army & American Character, 1775–1783*. Chapel Hill, NC: University of North Carolina Press.

Chapter 11

Crisis, Constitution, Nation: Probate Data and the Problem of Becoming American in the 1780s

Context

Here was a question that played on the minds of American leaders even before they had formally defeated the British, one that took on huge significance after Britain relinquished its claim to the American colonies in the Treaty of Paris in 1783: was one an American first, a Virginian first, or was there still a heavy dose of Britishness that would inform the new America if, in fact, there was to be one?

In a way, the Americans had answered this question themselves in the Declaration of Independence which referred explicitly not to *the* United States but to *these* colonies. The Declaration conceived not of one republic but rather a federation of individual republics. Yet this imagined nation begged questions. The Declaration proclaimed that the states were free and independent and had the power to levy war, conclude peace, contract alliances, and establish commerce. Did this mean that South Carolina, for example, as a free and independent state could sign a trade agreement with France, excluding the other states? What about dealing with other nations generally? What about lands to the west? If these territories were settled by Americans would they eventually join the United States? If so, how and in what capacity?

The answers to these questions lay in how the inhabitants of the thirteen former colonies would actually start to think of themselves as Americans. And on the surface, few things united them. They shared a common victory over a common enemy but was that enough to establish something other than local identity?

One answer came early after the signing of the Declaration when the states turned to drafting new state constitutions. Some basic ideas guided the new state constitutions. The people (at least white, male propertied ones), not a king or small cadre of aristocrats, should rule. Although most states did not alter their basic colonial governmental structure they did change the balance of power among the different branches of government. In general, they gave the executive branch very little power or abolished the office altogether. What the executives lost, the legislatures gained. The tendency was toward representativeness and they called for annual elections and required candidates for the legislature to live within the district they represented. And while no state granted universal manhood suffrage, most reduced the amount of property required of qualified voters.

While the states were busily drafting their constitutions, the national congress offered them the Articles of Confederation for ratification. The Congress approved these articles in November 1777 but it took four years for the states to ratify them. The Articles gave the national congress the authority to declare war and make peace, conduct diplomacy, coin money, and issue paper currency but it could not levy taxes or regulate trade. The power of the purse rested still with the states mainly because of the residual fear of a strong executive. Nor, according to the Articles, was there an executive branch. In other words, the Articles made the national congress very weak and these weaknesses would become apparent after the war had ended.

Winning independence from Britain only raised new questions, especially with regard to how best to govern. Perhaps the most pressing problem facing the new nation was economic. With the outbreak of war colonists suffered immediate economic loss. Formerly, Britain had supplied manufacturing goods, markets for American exports, and credit that enabled the colonial economy to flourish. The war changed all that. Southern planters were hit particularly hard because they had to seek new customers for their export staples as well as find new sources of capital but everyone suffered in some way.

Peace was costly. France and Britain flooded the American market with luxuries that a war weary American nation bought up. This spending left many individuals in debt. Local governments were also in debt from financing the war. In an effort to ameliorate state indebtedness, Congress and the states printed money but the only thing backing it was the government's promise to redeem the bills with money from future taxes which, of course, Congress was not in a position to levy. As a result, by 1781, paper money began to depreciate rapidly. Had Congress had the authority to stop the importation of goods, spending, and the outflow of capital, an inflationary spiral might have been prevented but without that authority, it could do little. States, on the other hand, responded to the economic crisis by printing more money. Congress could do nothing to stop them and so inflation mushroomed.

There were competing claims too in this inflationary economy. The rich wanted a strong currency backed by gold and silver (to deflate the economy) while the poor and middling classes – especially those in debt – wanted more paper money with which to pay their debts which, in turn, only aggravated inflationary tendencies. The social tensions that mounted during the 1780s became severe but, without a stronger congress, there was little that could be done.

As tension mounted between debtors and creditors, most notably in Shays's Rebellion (1786–7) centered in western Massachusetts where many small farmers were close to economic ruin, the need for a more robust framework of government became clear and, as a result, the Articles of Confederation were replaced with a new constitution which granted the national government considerable economic, diplomatic, and political authority. Written in 1787 and adopted by the states in 1788, the new Constitution was in place a year later. In 1791, the newly empowered Congress chartered the First Bank of the United States and, in effect, served as the country's treasury, allowing it to issue paper money, hopefully alleviate the economic problems that plagued the new republic, and basically wrested a great deal of fiscal and commercial authority from the states. The first American coins were struck in 1793 following the establishment of the US Mint.

On the surface, then, the United States Constitution not only established the political framework for protecting liberty, guaranteeing property, writing law, and administering and underwriting a qualified political democracy, it also gave a needed shot in the arm to the country's economy. But what of cultural and social identity? To what extent did Americans understand themselves as Americans, as part and parcel of a national identity, as Americans first and as, say, residents of Massachusetts second? And to what extent were there British legacies in the new republic? The document presented here offers a glimpse of how complicated and contingent becoming an American was, how, despite the Declaration of Independence and the War, old habits died hard, sometimes for good reason. The document also offers a glimpse of a future problem, one that would become sectional in nature between slaveholding and non-slaveholding states – the problem of slavery. Should human bondage, firmly entrenched in the southern states but beginning to evaporate in the northern ones, be allowed to flourish in the new republic, especially in a country supposedly dedicated to the promotion and preservation of liberty?

The document here – the only undated document in this collection – is suggestive. It is a probate record, a list of belongings and property with estimated values at the time of death, of John Evans of Charleston, South Carolina, one time clerk of the city's market. A close reading of the document is suggestive of not only the transition to an "American" nation but also telling of why slavery was to become such an important issue for the next seventy or so years.

Source

John Evans Probate Record, undated, Charleston Probate Inventory 1783–7, volume A, South Carolina Department of Archives and History, Columbia, South Carolina.[1]

11 Vd.
No. 27.

An Inventory and appraisement of the Goods & Chattels of the late Mr. John Evans (Clerk of the Market) deceased, vizt.

	Sterling		
Jacob, one Negro Boy £35 – Sophia a Wench 35	£ 70.	–	–
1 Pr. gold Sleeve Buttons, 1/2 doz Silver Tea Spoons & 1 Breast Pin 34/8 – 1 Pr. Stone Shoe Buckles, 1 Silver Watch 1 Seal 46/8 – 1 Silver Stock Buckle, 1 Pr. Silver Knee Buckles, 1 Pr. Silver Shoe do. 14/	4.	13.	4
1 Pr. Iron Dogs, 2 Clay Tea Pots & 1 Milk do. 1 Pr. Shovels 1 Tongs 9/4 – 1 Tea Kettle & Bellows, 1 close stool Pan 9/4 – 1 Mahogany Desk 65/3	4.	3.	11
1 Cypress Table, Pine Chest & black Trunk	1.	3.	4
1 small lot Queen's Ware, 1/2 doz Knives & Forks (buck handles) 7/ – An old Pavilion, 2 old Quilts, 1 Pr. old Sheets & 2 Blankets 18/8	1.	5.	8
2 Pillows, 4 Pillow Cases, a half finished Bed	3.	5.	3
1 Portuguese Cloak, 1 Pr. old Boots & 1 Suit blue Cloth	1.	17.	4
8 Pr. Cloth, Nankeen & Linnen Breeches	1.	17.	4
1 Suit black Princes Stuff, 10 Cloth & Linnen Jackets	2.	11.	4
7 Shirts, 1 coarse Sheet, 1 Napkin & 6 Pr. old Drawers	3.	14.	8
3 Hankfs. 2 Stocks 19 Pr. Thread worsted & silk Stockgs. & 5 Metal Spoons	3.	5.	4
Sterling £	97.	17.	6

Examined & Co. Sh. J.C. L.   George Warley – John Pomeroy – Bernard Moll

[To the student: use this page to transcribe the text of the document on the opposite page]

Study Questions

1. From what you have learned already, in which currency is the probate recorded?
2. Given that currency, when might you reasonably date the document? The probable date is in the note below. What does that probable date suggest about the transition from being a British colony to an American state?
3. What did John Evans possess? What proportion of his inventoried wealth was in slaves? What does that proportion suggest about the importance of slavery to a middling southerner (John Evans was not a planter) and how does it shed light on why slavery would become such a fractious issue in years to come?

Note

1. Although this probate is undated, we know from other sources that John Evans of Charleston, South Carolina, died on January 28, 1785 and it is likely that the probate record dates from the same year. See Caroline T. Moore, ed., *Abstracts of Wills of Charleston District South Carolina and Other Wills Recorded in the District 1783–1800* (Columbia, SC: The R. L. Bryan Company, 1974), p. 83.

Further Reading

Amar, Akhil Reed 2005: *America's Constitution: A Biography.* New York: Random House.

Bowen, Catherine Drinker 1986: *Miracle at Philadelphia: The Story of the Constitutional Convention May to September, 1787.* Boston, MA: Little, Brown and Company.

Burns, James MacGregor 1982: *The Vineyard of Liberty: The American Experiment.* New York: Alfred A. Knopf.

Hoffert, Robert W. 1992: *A Politics of Tensions: The Articles of Confederation and American Political Ideas.* Niwot, CO: University Press of Colorado.

Jensen, Merrill 1970: *The Articles of Confederation: An Interpretation of the Social-Constitutional History of the American Revolution 1774–1781.* Madison, WI: University of Wisconsin Press.

Morris, Richard B. 1987: *The Forging of the Union, 1781–1789.* New York: Harper and Row.

Rakove, Jack N. 1996: *Original Meanings: Politics and Ideas in the Making of the Constitution.* New York: Alfred Knopf.

Robinson, Donald L. 1970: *Slavery in the Structure of American Politics, 1765–1820.* New York: Harcourt Brace Jovanovich.

Smith, Craig R. 1993: *To Form a More Perfect Union: the Ratification of the Constitution and the Bill of Rights, 1787–1791.* Lanham, MD: University Press of America.

Wood, Gordon S. 1969: *The Creation of the American Republic, 1776–1787.* Chapel Hill, NC: University of North Carolina Press.

Chapter 12

The New Republic: A Massachusetts Federalist in 1800

Context

In 1790, America's population was overwhelmingly rural: there were only 24 towns and cities of more than 2,500 people and the vast majority of Americans lived outside the cities where they engaged in agriculture. In such a rural environment, the movement of goods, people, and information was slow. Few people used the relatively expensive postal system and most roads were little more than cleared paths. The ninety or so newspapers in circulation infrequently made their way into the most rural parts of America and were read, instead, principally by residents of cities. These cities, by contrast, were cosmopolitan, information-oriented, and connected to the outside world through trade.

Rural/urban distinctions were important in the new republic. In rural America in 1790, wealth was spread fairly broadly and subsistence was the goal of most white families. They tended to use the labor of the entire family and sell goods on a market only when they produced a surplus. Wealth in cities was far more concentrated in the hands of fewer people and urban inhabitants tended to be more commercially oriented.

These differences held important implications for the political evolution of the new republic. Indeed, the very debate over the ratification of the Constitution reflected these differences. Urban merchants, workers, and commercial farmers generally rallied behind ratification. They took a broader, more cosmopolitan view of the nation's future and viewed a stronger federal government favorably, especially since they believed a more muscular national congress would be instrumental in bolstering trade and commerce. Rural, subsistence Americans tended to oppose the Constitution or were at least lukewarm to it. They feared concentrated power and were particularly suspicious of commercial institutions which they thought had played a major part in undermining American liberty during the crisis of the 1760s. Although they were a majority of the population, they were scattered and not easily mobilized.

Whatever forms the tensions between these groups would assume, there was general agreement immediately after the war that George Washington should lead it. He was elected unanimously and in second place came John Adams who, according to the terms of the Constitution, served as Vice President. Washington's two most important cabinet appointments were Alexander Hamilton as Secretary of the Treasury and Thomas Jefferson as head of the State Department, two men who, in many ways, represented the differences between urban, commercial America (Hamilton) and rural, subsistence-oriented America (Jefferson).

Asked by Congress to prepare a report on the nation's finances, Hamilton aimed to use the power of the federal government to encourage manufacturing and commerce in an effort to make the United States economically independent of Europe. He was also interested in tying the interests of the wealthy to those of the new government, giving them a vested stake in the new republic. Neither goal could be achieved until Hamilton solved two pressing problems facing the new government: how to raise revenue and restore credit in order to convince merchants and foreign nations that the United States government would pay its debts. Hamilton proposed to fund (pay) all $52 million of the federal debt and recommended that the federal government assume responsibility for the $25 million in debt that individual states owed. He aimed to pay for all of this by levying taxes on certain items, especially on imported manufactures, which, in turn, he hoped would protect and stimulate American industry.

Although extremely controversial, in 1791 funding and assumption passed Congress, as did Hamilton's recommendation for a charter for the first Bank of the United States which would hold government deposits and issue banknotes that would be received in payment of all debts owed the government. The controversy and debate was revealing and helped stimulate the development of two political parties (although, initially, they were more like factions and highly fugitive and malleable groups), the Federalists (embodied by Hamilton) and the Democratic-Republicans (headed by James Madison and Thomas Jefferson). The Democratic-Republican Party was also known as the Republican Party, although it has no connection to the modern party of the same name.

To the Republicans, it seemed as though the Hamiltonian-Federalist program promoted the commercial sector at the expense of semi-subsistence farmers, thereby establishing a privileged class who would benefit from the federal underwriting of funding, assumption, and the establishment of the National Bank. To Jefferson especially, this smacked of the old corrupt, English system where politics and commercial interests were tightly interwoven. Desirous of a more broadly based democratic system, many Republicans believed that Hamilton's policies favored urban environments and was but one step removed from making cities and their citizens dependent on the vagaries of commerce and wage labor. For Madison and Jefferson, such schemes were incompatible with liberty which they considered grounded in, and safeguarded by, land ownership, the only sure guarantee of republican independence.

The Federalists and Republicans further defined their ideologies and emerging party consciousness in the 1790s over a variety of issues including the French Revolution (which the Federalists, ever fearful of excessive democracy, derided and which the Republicans, self-styled friends of liberty, supported). In 1796, the weary George Washington, tired of inter-party bickering, announced he would not run for a third term and in his farewell address warned against the dangers of partyism. In a very close election, John Adams (Federalist) beat Jefferson. The election showed much about party identity and support. Geographically, federalism was strongest in New England and other areas, including regions of the plantation South that enjoyed strong commercial ties with the United Kingdom. Republicans, on the other hand, won most of their support in agricultural areas where subsistence was common and where extensive commercial ties were weak. Urban workers, recent immigrants, and some small shopkeepers also supported the Republicans because they disliked the aristocratic tone of the Federalists.

Adams faced several problems during his presidency. Rancorous debate over immigration especially sharpened party identities. In 1798 Congress passed the Alien and Sedition Acts, the former authorizing the arrest and deportation of aliens suspected of treasonable activities. Although never used, the Act directly threatened non-naturalized immigrants – most of whom supported the Republican Party. The Act also increased the period of residence required to become a naturalized citizen from 5 to 14 years – again, to limit the number of Republican voters. Even more controversial was the Sedition Act which imposed heavy fines and imprisonment for writing, speaking, or publishing anything deemed of a false, scandalous, and malicious nature against the government. A number of Republican newspapers were closed or censored as a result. The Federalists proved heavy handed and their efforts to stifle their opposition failed. In 1800, Thomas Jefferson became President and inaugurated a new era in which many of his ideas and principles would hold sway.

Yet it is easy to simply caricature the political philosophies of both parties. Within each of their ranks were men of diverse opinion, cherishing some aspects of their party's core beliefs but critical of others. Jefferson, for example, even though a vehement champion of democracy and leery of manufactures, became quite pragmatic on economic matters and even ended up abetting the Hamiltonian penchant for territorial expansion with the Louisiana Purchase in 1803. Likewise, Federalists were not of common mind on all matters. This following letter suggests as much. It was written by Fisher Ames, an ardent Massachusetts

Federalist and one of the most eloquent orators of his day. Ames was drawn to federalism because of its unapologetically elite characteristics and a belief in a natural aristocracy, the rule of the most talented. He was also extremely fearful of tyranny but located its source principally in the tyranny of the majority and what he believed were the mobocratic tendencies of the Democratic-Republicans. He feared that the Jacobinism or radical democracy of the French Revolution would be imported into the United States and this worry made him especially critical of Thomas Jefferson, whom he understood as a champion of radical democracy. Ames doubted that people were sufficiently virtuous and imbued with public morality to exercise the privilege of democracy. But he was also critical of some Federalist initiatives and opposed the Hamiltonian quest for territorial and economic expansion. In this letter, he expresses some of his views immediately after the election of 1800 to Henry Van Schaack, a well-known western Massachusetts Federalist whose antipathy toward the Revolutionary War was well known.

Source

Fisher Ames to Mr [Henry] Van Schaack, Boston, March 7, 1801, Papers of Fisher Ames, Manuscript Division, Library of Congress, Washington, DC.

Boston March 7th 1801

My dear Sir

I offer you my best thanks for your polite and very entertaining letter, and I am the more indebted to you for the invitation to your house as I think I shd be more welcome there than some of the people's present royal family – a distinction conferred that is justly flattering to my vanity. The honest federalists are to have little other consolation in future, if we may trust the democratic soothsayers, than their mutual esteem and regard. They the Democrats are audacious and busy beyond former example, and make a mockery of all our efforts to keep the state powers out of their hands.

Two causes make our affairs turbulent. The ambition of Virginia to rule the U. States, and the spirit of jacobinism. These two coincide in Virginia but only the latter ought to have influence among our yankee levellers. They generally expect to see trade and manufactures cherished and protected and a navy maintained. There is ground enough for a jealousy of Virginia but it is not yet perceived ....

my dear Sir, with respect and esteem

yrs sincerely

Fisher Ames

Mr Vanschaack

[To the student: use this page to transcribe the text of the document on the opposite page]

Study Questions

1. What is Ames' attitude toward democracy? Is the personal also political for Ames?
2. In what ways does Ames seem to differ from the Hamiltonian style of federalism?
3. Suggest reasons why Ames is so concerned about Virginia.

Further Reading

Appleby, Joyce 1984: *Capitalism and a New Social Order: The Republican Vision of the 1790s*. New York: New York University Press.

Banning, Lance 1978: *The Jeffersonian Persuasion: Evolution of a Party Ideology.* Ithaca, NY: Cornell University Press.

Huston, James L. 1993: The American Revolutionaries, the Political Economy of Aristocracy, and the American Concept of the Distribution of Wealth, 1765–1900. 98 *American Historical Review*, 1075–105.

Kloppenberg, James T. 1987: The Virtues of Liberalism: Christianity, Republicanism, and Ethics in Early American Political Discourse. 74 *Journal of American History*, 9–33.

McCoy, Drew 1982: *The Elusive Republic: Political Economy in Jeffersonian America*. Chapel Hill, NC: University of North Carolina Press.

McDonald, Forrest 1979: *Alexander Hamilton: A Biography.* New York: W. W. Norton and Company.

Miller, John C. 1960: *The Federalist Era, 1789–1800*. New York: HarperCollins.

Wood, Gordon S. 1987: Ideology and the Origins of Liberal America. 44 *William and Mary Quarterly*, 628–40.

Chapter 13

Jeffersonian America: On the Road in 1818

Context

Jeffersonian America was a feeling more than it was a strictly demarcated presidential administration. Beginning in 1801, Thomas Jefferson served two terms and was followed by fellow Republicans, James Madison and James Monroe, both of whom perpetuated basic Jeffersonian ideas about America's future well into the 1820s. More than that, Jefferson, Madison, and, to some extent, Monroe, presided over a period in American history that saw the new nation begin to move westward and experience the problems of slavery and sectional consciousness.

Yet Jeffersonian America, while qualitatively different from the Federalist program, was a complicated ideological and political landscape and Jefferson in particular found it difficult to cleave precisely to his own ideology of limited state intervention in the economy, scaled-back claims concerning territorial aggrandizement, and the promotion of agriculture rather than the sponsorship of industry, commerce, and manufacturing. Jefferson inherited a reality that required him to compromise, to offer pragmatic solutions, to work within parameters while not sacrificing wholly his vision of an American future grounded in republican simplicity and virtue.

On some matters, Jefferson radically revised Federalist policy. He did away with Hamilton's internal taxes and radically reduced the size of the military. Yet even here, such actions helped in part reduce the national debt, something that would have earned Hamilton's applause. Jefferson also allowed the National Bank to persist, arguing that it should run its course until its charter expired in 1811.

Westward expansion also offered a mixed bag. Many Federalists had viewed the selling of western lands as a way to generate revenue to support the commercial aspirations of the country. Jefferson, on the other hand, understood western lands as a way to preserve the values of an agrarian republic. America's vast lands would allow men and women to leave cities in the East and establish rural independence, free from the corrupting tendencies of urban, commercial life. In other words, Jefferson and his followers saw westward expansion as a way to preserve republican virtue in time, for future generations. This philosophy helps explain why Jefferson felt comfortable with the Louisiana Purchase of 1803 which doubled the size of the United States for the bargain price of $15 million. The Federalists happily pointed out the inconsistency in the acquisition of the territory from France. Jefferson, who had always argued that the Constitution should be interpreted in a terse, strict fashion, could not square this circle – the Constitution did not grant the President explicit powers to buy foreign territory. Jefferson countered by arguing that the larger concern with the preservation of American liberty, something he believed the Purchase would achieve, overrode such a technicality.

Yet acquiring such a huge piece of land and settling it did involve some compromise on Jefferson's part. Following the Purchase, Americans began to move westward with enthusiasm. Although Jefferson was jittery about federal sponsorship of anything smacking of commerce and emerging manufacturing he gave in to the manifest need to begin to link his sprawling country. When Ohio became a state in 1803, preliminary legislation providing for a National Road was considered by Congress which directed that a proportion of the money derived from land sales in Ohio go toward the construction of a road linking the east coast, through Ohio to the Midwest. Construction of the National Road began in 1811, once Jefferson had authorized a survey of the land and seven years later, in 1818, the road ran from Cumberland, Maryland to Wheeling, Virginia, on the Ohio River.

Jefferson also found that he could not avoid dealing with the wider world. Two weeks after the French agreed to the Louisiana Purchase, another war broke out between Britain and France. Jefferson attempted to keep the United States neutral but this proved increasingly difficult as the British began to seize American ships, impress American sailors, and even fired on an American ship in US waters in June 1807. Instead of declaring war, Jefferson opted for a policy of "peaceable coercion," one designed to protect American neutral rights without entering a costly war. Peaceable coercion took the form of the Embargo Act of 1807 which prohibited American ships from trading with foreign ports and halted the export of US goods. Jefferson thought American markets and exports were sufficiently important to both warring powers that Britain and France would respect American neutrality. He was wrong. Neither nation was as dependent on the US as Jefferson thought. US exports plunged from $108 million in 1807 to $22 million in 1808; imports similarly plummeted. Americans, not the British or French, were hurt the most. Ironically, however, the Embargo Act may have helped spur US manufacturing, at least in the intermediate term, something Jefferson had always wanted to avoid. According to some historians, the Act might have had the effect of internalizing capital that would otherwise have been spent on British manufactures. The availability of capital within the United States led to investment in US manufacturing, something very close to Hamilton's heart but anathema to Jefferson.

Jefferson left office and James Madison assumed responsibility for dealing with Britain and France. The failure of peaceable coercion combined with continuing British hostility led Madison to declare war against Britain, something every Federalist voted against. The United States was not in a strong position to fight the War of 1812 against Britain and the American victory in 1815 was of some surprise to European powers generally. This victory, combined with the nationalistic upsurge accompanying it, dealt a severe blow to the Federalist Party (which was perceived as disloyal) and enabled the Republicans to win handily the 1816 election.

James Monroe, the new President, presided over a period in which America turned toward domestic issues while shoring up its international authority. Domestically, this period saw the emergence of the slavery issue – where should slavery be permitted? – and resolved, at least for the time being, in the Missouri Compromise of 1820 which, in essence, banned slavery north of the 36 degree and 30 minute line in territory west from Missouri to the Rocky Mountains and allowed slavery south of it. In 1823, Monroe issued the Monroe Doctrine stating that while the United States would not intervene in European affairs, it would resent any European intervention in the new republics of Latin America, thereby positioning the United States as the main authority in the Americas.

Jeffersonian America, then, was a time of expansion and of consolidation, of peace and war, of unity and diversity. These themes engaged many Americans and even as they traveled they discussed them. The following is an excerpt from a travel diary kept by Samuel Whitcomb of Massachusetts. Whitcomb was a traveling book salesman and ventured throughout the Midwest and South. In 1818, he kept a fairly detailed, if scribbled, diary. We meet him while he is traveling in the vicinity of Wheeling, Virginia (later, West Virginia) on the Ohio River. This diary entry is made on July 5, 1818. The "N. Worsestor" to whom he refers was Noah Worcester of New Hampshire, a noted Unitarian clergyman and the co-founder of the American peace movement.

Source

Samuel Whitcomb diaries, 1818–45, Samuel Whitcomb papers, Diary for 1818, Ms. N-265, Massachusetts Historical Society, Boston, Massachusetts.

... it killed by accidental ...

The people of Ohio are accused of countenancing the runingaway of Slaves. & many are lost from this vicinity, by that means 'tis said. Yankees appear to be generally despised in this part of the country. Ignorance & vice are but too evident characteristics of many of the River Inhabitants there are however some pleasing exceptions. The House where we staid night before the last was an example of hospitality, & religion. We find ourselves well situated this morng. — Afternoon. This forenoon went to meeting & heard a Methodist (in the Court House) declaim against Unitarianism. He undertook to state N. Worcester's scheme but made poor work of it. how absurd it ~~[illegible]~~ to hear people addressed in such strains on subjects they know nothing! — A Kentucky Boat has just came down the river. It is the one from which a young man was drowned day before yesterday. Several of the men stood on the top rowing — in their shirt flaps. I have ~~frequently~~ seen them — without any shirts on — only pantaloons — these had no pants only Hats & Shirts! No meeting here this afternoon. Something like a holiday. I had like to have come down in the Kentucky Boat myself. —

[To the student: use this page to transcribe the text of the document on the opposite page]

Study Questions

1. What is the general tone of the diary entry? Does it depict the region as sluggish and stagnant or energized and full of movement?
2. Is there evidence in the excerpt to suggest emerging sectional and regional differences in America?
3. What sort of intellectual issues had currency at the time of the diary entry?

Further Reading

Dangerfield, George 1965: *The Awakening of American Nationalism, 1815–1828*. New York: Harper and Row.

Ellis, Richard E. 1974: *The Jeffersonian Crisis: Courts and Politics in the Early Republic*. New York: Norton.

Freeman, Joanne 2001: *Affairs of Honor: National Politics in the New Republic*. New Haven: Yale University Press.

McCoy Drew 1982: *The Elusive Republic: Political Economy in Jeffersonian America*. Chapel Hill, NC: University of North Carolina Press.

Peterson, Merrill 1970: *Thomas Jefferson and the New Nation: A Biography.* New York: Oxford University Press.

Ratcliffe, Donald 1998: *Party Spirit in a Frontier Republic: Democratic Politics in Ohio, 1793–1821*. Columbus, OH: Ohio State University Press.

Smelser, Marshall 1968: *The Democratic Republic, 1801–1815*. New York: Harper and Row.

Spivak, Burton 1979: *Jefferson's English Crisis: Commerce, the Embargo, and the Republican Revolution*. Charlottesville, VA: University Press of Virginia.

Watts, Steven 1987: *The Republic Reborn: War and the Making of Liberal America, 1790–1820*. Baltimore, MD: The Johns Hopkins University Press.

Chapter 14

Revolutions in Time and Space: Tourism and Travel, 1850

Context

One of the ostensible paradoxes of the history of the United States from roughly 1790 to 1860 is that as the country grew in geographic size it became an increasingly smaller place. In 1800, for example, it took about two weeks to travel from New York City to Charleston, South Carolina; by 1857 it took just two days. Information, goods, people, all could be moved with much greater efficiency and speed as the period wore on. What some historians consider a "Market Revolution" was critical for binding the expanding country together. But a tighter country did not necessarily mean a more unified one, as we will see in coming chapters.

A national system of markets began to emerge following the War of 1812. It was a domestic network stimulated by a series of "internal improvements," or what some historians have termed a "transport revolution." Prior to the War of 1812, trade within the United States was limited principally to the coast and tied to international markets; after the war until the outbreak of the Civil War in 1861, the United States consolidated its internal market. In this period, the cost of transportation on land fell by about half while its speed increased almost fivefold.

Canals were important to the process. Perhaps the most famous, and one that helped stimulate a spate of canal building nationally, was the Erie Canal, stretching 364 miles from Albany to Buffalo and built between 1818 and 1825. The canal reduced the cost of shipping a ton of goods from Buffalo to New York City from more than 19 cents a mile to less than 3 cents a mile within a few years of its completion. It also stimulated economic growth in other ways. Not only did the Erie canal inspire other states to construct canals but towns developed alongside it, creating nodes of economic activity. By 1840, the United States had about 3,000 miles of canals supported by a mix of private and state monies.

The development of riparian and ocean-going steamboats was also critical for reducing travel time. Steamboats were able to plow upstream on the Mississippi with increasing frequency and the fleet of ocean-going steamboats that hop-scotched their way down the east coast was immensely important for linking North and South economically. The emergence of better, macadamized roads was also important to the transport revolution.

But nothing quite approached the railroads. The railroad's speed – very modest by today's standard, of course – was nonetheless extraordinary for antebellum Americans and its temporal precision, relative independence from the weather, and rapid development throughout the United States earned much public and private commentary.

The numbers are impressive. In 1830, the nation had a paltry 13 miles of track; by 1840, railroad and canal mileage was on rough par at just over 3,000 miles; by 1850, the country boasted nearly 9,000 miles of track. Southern states were as much involved in railroad development as northern ones. In fact, in the mid 1830s, the Charleston and Hamburg Railroad was the world's longest (136 miles) under single management, connecting the state's interior cotton plantations to the port of Charleston. It was also the first to experiment with using standard time, something that did not gain national foothold until long after the Civil War.

Combined, the transport revolution linked previously isolated markets to the national market and, as a result, formerly self-sufficient farmers could now grow crops for cash. This, in turn, stimulated demand for banks and merchants. But agriculture was not the only sector affected. If cotton and corn could be transported, so too could information, and, increasingly, it was as the United States postal service became braided with the emerging transportation system. The postal system made especially good use of ships and the railroad in particular. They contracted with railroad companies to deliver the mail at various locations punctually and regularly and thereby helped make the communication of information efficient and affordable. In the process, people from one part of the expanding country learned, via letter, newspaper, and magazine, what was occurring in another part and began to participate in a maturing imagined American community that augmented American nationalism and proved increasingly important to commercial interests. By 1828, there were five times as many post offices in the United States as there were in Britain.

Americans who could afford to travel also began to engage in tourism and leisure. Sights, smells, sounds, and places only once imagined could now be experienced, consumed, and then relived through the increasingly popular practice of collecting souvenirs. As northerners visited the South and as increasing numbers of southerners ventured northward, sectional stereotypes were both betrayed by actual experience and, sometimes, reaffirmed. The market and transport revolutions highlighted sectional similarities and differences and were surely a factor in both postponing and, eventually, actuating the outbreak of sectional hostilities in 1861.

None of this would have happened, however, without some important political and legal developments. The "New Nationalism" of influential leaders such as Henry Clay, John C. Calhoun, and John Quincy Adams fostered a set of economic policies designed to bind the country together. Perhaps of even greater import were a series of Supreme Court decisions during Chief Justice John Marshall's term (1801–35). He was convinced that the Supreme Court should uphold the sanctity of private property and that the power of the federal government could be used profitably to promote economic growth. To that end, the Supreme Court upheld the constitutionality of the Second Bank of the United States (*McCulloch v. Maryland*, 1803),[1] promoted the federal government's right to regulate interstate commerce (*Gibbons v. Ogden*, 1824),[2] and defined the nature of contract law and established the preeminence of private property (*Fletcher v. Peck*, 1810).[3] All in all, the Supreme Court facilitated the expansion of the economy and greased the wheels of the market revolution by encouraging economic risk taking, protecting property, limiting state interference in business, and fostering a climate of business confidence.

How individuals experienced the emerging market revolution varied, of course. For many Americans, it would still take years for them to become incorporated into transportation networks. But for others, the ties that increasingly bound America were felt quite keenly. Not only did people from one region of the country increasingly have (relatively) easy access to other areas, but the very process of getting there – and back – instilled new habits of travel. Presented here is a portion of an 1850 letter from Mary Jones in Philadelphia to her sons (one of whom was to become an influential Presbyterian minister, educator, and planter in Georgia) who were attending college at Princeton University. Superficially, the letter simply recounts her travel experiences, detailing happenings and events, some of them quite mundane. But a close reading suggests something about not only the newly emerging habits and discipline of travel but also about the growing ease of travel not just for business but also for leisure.

Source

Letter from Mary Jones (in Philadelphia) to "My very dear Sons" (C. C., Jr., and Joseph, who are in school at Princeton), October 7, 1850, Folder 7, Box 2 of the Charles Colcock Jones collection, Hargrett Library, University of Georgia.

Philadelphia October 7th 1850.

My very dear Sons,

We left our quiet home at May-bank on the morning of the 1st which was Tuesday of last week - arrived in Savannah about 5 o'clk took tea - after which, your Aunt & Cousins - Father Sister & myself started in the Omnibus for the Steam-boat Wharf - where we were kept waiting for the Duncan Clinch until after ten o'clk the Boat being occupied until that hour bringing in passengers from the Isabel - one of the West India Steamers lying in the offing - We soon fired up & with a sad heart I bade adieu to my own native State - I could not trust myself to express the feelings which had all day possessed my mind - but I hope it was in humble faith that we com-mitted our bodies & our spirits - and all our future prospects - for time & for Eternity - to God who hath a right to us, and all we possess. - In consequence of our late start we did not reach Charleston before 12 o'clk, dined at the Planter's Hotel & left at 3 o'clk in the Gladiator - we had a fine run all night - and reached Wilmington by 1/2 past 7 o'clk - where we took a walk and

[To the student: use this page to transcribe the text of the document on the opposite page]

Study Questions

1. How might we characterize Mary Jones's perception of time and what role might the transport revolution have played in shaping that perception? How might perceptions of time have changed from, say, a century earlier?
2. Is there evidence in the letter of the juxtaposition of "modern" and "traditional" attitudes? Did travel inspire confidence? Did it require the virtue of patience?
3. How might a travelogue, written today, differ from Mary Jones's and why?

Notes

1. *McCulloch v. Maryland*, 4 Wheat. (17 U.S.) 316 (1819).
2. *Gibbons v. Ogden*, 4 Wheat. (22 U.S.) 1 (1824).
3. *Fletcher v. Peck*, 6 Cranch (10 U.S.) 87 (1810).

Further Reading

Hawke, David Freeman 1988: *Nuts and Bolts of the Past: A History of American Technology, 1776–1860*. New York: Harper and Row.

John, Richard R. 1998: *Spreading the News: The American Postal System from Franklin to Morse*. Cambridge, MA: Harvard University Press.

Larson, John Lauritz 2001: *Internal Improvement: National Public Works and the Promise of Popular Government in the Early United States*. Chapel Hill, NC: University of North Carolina Press.

O'Malley, Michael 1990: *Keeping Watch: A History of Time in America*. New York: Viking.

Sears, John F. 1989: *Sacred Places: American Tourist Attractions in the Nineteenth Century*. Amherst, MA: University of Massachusetts Press.

Sellers, Charles G. 1991: *The Market Revolution: Jacksonian America, 1815–1848*. New York: Oxford University Press.

Sheriff, Carol 1996: *The Artificial River: The Erie Canal and the Paradox of Progress, 1817–1862*. New York: Hill and Wang.

Smith, Mark M. 1997: *Mastered by the Clock: Time, Slavery and Freedom in the America South*. Chapel Hill, NC: University of North Carolina Press.

Taylor, George R. 1951: *The Transportation Revolution: 1815–1860*. New York: Holt, Rinehart and Winston.

Chapter 15

The Age of Jackson: The View from Abroad in 1828

Context

The Age of Jackson started with a political loss for the former general and hero of the War of 1812. James Monroe did not run in the election of 1824 and instead the leaders of the Republican Party, via a caucus, selected Secretary of the Treasury William H. Crawford of Georgia as their presidential nominee. But three other Republicans considered the caucus system undemocratic and they decided to run also, ignoring the caucus' choice of Crawford. These men were new republicans, men of an ardent nationalist stripe: Secretary of State John Quincy Adams; John C. Calhoun (Monroe's Secretary of War); Henry Clay, the Speaker of the House; and Andrew Jackson.

Initially, few politicians took Jackson's candidacy for the party's nomination seriously. He was politically inexperienced and known mainly for his military endeavors. But as Jackson gained popular support from the West and the South, savvy politicians began to gravitate toward him. In the election itself, no one received a majority of the popular vote. Calhoun stepped out of the race; Clay received 37 Electoral College votes, Crawford 41, Adams 84, with Jackson heading the list with 99 votes. At this point, the proceedings became murky and Henry Clay stepped in using his considerable influence as Speaker of the House (constitutionally, the House of Representatives had authority to select the top candidates). Clay had a private meeting with Adams, rallied the House behind him, and caused Adams to win. That Clay would be his new Secretary of State (a position at the time often thought of as the first stepping stone to the Presidency) was among Adams' first announcements as President. Jackson and his supporters termed this the "Corrupt Bargain" and, since Jackson campaigned heavily in 1828 on this theme of anticorruption and prodemocracy, in a way, the race for the next presidency was already underway in 1824.

The election of 1824 was significant in other respects, most notably in the way it changed the old party system. Clay and Adams began to organize a new party known as the National Republicans to distinguish themselves from Jefferson's old Republican Party (which was less national in view and less friendly toward economic development than Clay and Adams would have liked). Jackson and his supporters began to call themselves the Democrats, a label intended to convey their belief in participatory democracy, their appeal to the "common man," and their rejection of economic and political elitism, which they believed had begun to dominate the country.

Jackson and the Democrats did, in fact, both capture and help promote something of a new political culture in America, especially following Jackson's successful campaign in 1828. For the first time, large numbers of Americans saw politics as relevant to their lives. Many states, north and south, opened up the political process, some eliminating property qualifications for voting and allowing most white adult males to vote. Similarly, property requirements for holding political office were either dropped or reduced. As a result, elections became the means through which white men expressed their policy preferences by voting for candidates pledged to specific programs. These developments in turn gave rise to a new type of politician – the party politician, a man devoted to party service who depended on public office for his livelihood, one often drawn from the middling ranks of society who knew how to conduct a mass campaign to get his party into office.

The effect was quantitative and qualitative. In the 1824 Presidential election, 27 percent of eligible voters went to the polls; in 1828, 56 percent did. By 1840, the figure was 78 percent. Moreover, there was an emerging sense of political engagement. Political rallies grew in frequency and size, often raucous and animated; grassroots political campaigning became increasingly popular; and, on the whole, eligible voters seemed to become heavily invested in the outcome of political contests. We should not be misled into thinking this was pure democracy at work – after all, women and slaves could not vote – but it gave the period a democratic spirit, a trait often recognized by foreign visitors to the United States in the 1830s.

If the Jacksonian Democrats stood for democracy, a powerful Executive, a modern, forward-looking political consciousness, and a sometimes backward view of the economy painting commercial interests and manufacturing as threatening to individual liberty and independence, their opposition, the Whig Party, founded in 1833, stood in stark contrast and helped animate political contests. Specifically, the Whigs, counting Henry Clay, Daniel Webster, and a young Abraham Lincoln in their fold, were critical of Jackson because they believed he was inaugurating an irresponsible, boisterous democratic ethos in America, one in which mobocracy and unrestrained, irresponsible, and socially destructive strains would undermine sober, sensible political leadership. More inclined to look wistfully back to a political order of the past in which political and social deference guided elections, the Whigs were also ardent modernizers, anxious to promote economic development and tie the fortunes of the federal government to that development.

Such ideological distinctions became apparent over lots of issues, but particularly over banking, which reveals a great deal about Jackson's lack of understanding of financial matters and his appeal to the masses. In 1823 Nicholas Biddle, a wealthy businessman from Philadelphia, was appointed President of the National Bank. His aim, simply, was to restore the Bank's reputation following some severe fiscal panics (especially that of 1819) and to do so he set out to use the Bank to regulate the amount of credit available in the economy, especially that issued by state banks. If Biddle believed that a state bank was over-extended – that it had issued more paper notes than was prudent – he asked that bank to redeem the value of its paper notes in specie (gold or silver). If banks did not have enough specie reserves to back all the paper money they had issued, the only way a bank could redeem its notes was to call in its loans, reduce the amount of notes in circulation, and thereby lessen the amount of credit in the economy and, from Biddle's perspective, dampening inflation and keeping the economy sound.

Biddle made the National Bank extremely powerful and the darling of commercial and business interests. Jackson, himself indebted early in his life and concerned about the power of business, had grave reservations about the Bank and Biddle's running of it. During the election of 1832, Biddle called for an early renewal of the Bank's charter (which was due to expire in 1836) and Jackson made this a central point of his campaign. He vetoed Congressional efforts to renew the charter, arguing that the Bank was an agent of special privilege and damaging to agricultural interests. Jackson won the 1832 election handily and his victory renewed his determination to not only not recharter the Bank but destroy it. He succeeded and after 1836 no national bank existed. His actions proved catastrophic. State banks now ran the economy, issued too many loans, over-extended credit, and inflated the economy, all of which led to one of the most pronounced financial crises in the nation's history in 1839. Jackson's deep dislike of commercial interests, his belief that the Bank damaged the common man, and his almost intuitive repulsion at government-sponsored economic development left the country in a deep recession that lasted into the 1840s.

Unsurprisingly, then, not everyone was enamored of the Age of Jackson and even at its very dawn, some Americans clearly entertained reservations about the emerging direction and nature of American society. Excerpted here is a letter written by William R. Lawrence of Massachusetts to his father, Amos Lawrence, from Paris, right after Jackson's election in 1828. The view from abroad helps place Jackson's election and the broader culture emerging in the United

States during the late 1820s in clear relief and Lawrence happily expresses his views on the tenor of US society. Clearly, Jackson's election was important news but, perhaps more important, we gain insight to the mind of men who were likely to resist the general tendencies of Jacksonian America.

Source

William R. Lawrence, Paris, to his father, February 5, 1829, William R. Lawrence Letterbooks, third journal, pp. 9–10, Massachusetts Historical Society, Boston, Massachusetts.

Situated as I am in a foreign Country, the greatest pleasure one has, is in reading letters and papers from home: in regard to the latter I have a pretty liberal store, as Mr. Draper takes the principal newspapers that are printed in New York and Boston, and lends them to me. General Jackson is to be the next President, which is the only new thing of much importance in the late papers.

In Paris the papers are very small, and have not much in them concerning politics, or any thing else of importance; The Frenchman does not concern himself much about political affairs, only now and then to write a piece concerning some new minister. They have the name of being honest, but their honesty consists in this; If you leave your handkerchief upon their Counter, they will restore it to you; but if you go into a store and ask the price of an article, he will always demand two or three times the value of the thing, and if you will not give it, he will lower until he comes to a just price; He has no fixed price for his articles, but demands according to the appearance of the buyer, if he is a foreigner they will impose upon him as much as possible; they have a great deal of politeness but it is only studied,

[To the student: use this page to transcribe the text of the document on the opposite page]

for while he bows and takes off his hat with one hand, he will pick your pocket with the other; This is the general opinion of them, by all the foreigners with whom I have conversed, who judge probably rather severely of them being the subjects of their impositions. They are not however so noisy and quarrelsome as in America, which is in their favor; at all the public places the greatest order prevails, and you never see any of those noisy quarrelsome fellows, that so disgrace some places in America.

The police of Paris is one of the finest in the world; it is composed of a great number of armed and mounted men, who are continually traversing the city; besides these, there are a great number of foot soldiers, taken from the regular army; to keep order at the Theatres alone, employs twelve hundred men; riots and mobs are seldom seen; if so, they are put down by martial law. One riot was attempted a year or two since, but the police turned out and shot nearly an hundred persons.

[To the student: use this page to transcribe the text of the document on the opposite page]

Study Questions

1. What, in Lawrence's opinion, were the main differences between Americans and the French?
2. Do you detect a relationship between social manners and political persuasion from this letter?
3. Do you think Lawrence was more likely to support the Whig or Democratic Party? Justify your answer.

Further Reading

Altschuler, Glenn C. and Stuart Blumin 2000: *Rude Republic: Americans and Their Politics in the Nineteenth Century.* Princeton, NJ: Princeton University Press.

Baker, Jean 1983: *Affairs of Party: The Political Culture of Northern Democrats in the Mid-Nineteenth Century.* Ithaca, NY: Cornell University Press.

Cole, Donald B. 1993: *The Presidency of Andrew Jackson.* Lawrence, KA: University Press of Kansas.

Ellis, Richard 1987: *The Union at Risk: Jacksonian Democracy, States Rights, and the Nullification Crisis.* New York: Oxford University Press.

Feller, Daniel 1995: *The Jacksonian Promise: America, 1815–1840.* Baltimore, MD: The Johns Hopkins University Press.

Formisano, Ronald 1983: *The Transformation of Political Culture: Massachusetts Parties, 1790s–1840s.* New York: Oxford University Press.

Holt, Michael P. 2003: *The Rise and Fall of the American Whig Party: Jacksonian Politics and the Onset of the Civil War.* New York: Oxford University Press.

Kohl, Lawrence F. 1989: *The Politics of Individualism: Parties and the American Character in the Jackson Era.* New York: Oxford University Press.

Ryan, Mary P. 1998: *Civic Wars: Democracy and Public Life in the American City during the Nineteenth Century.* Berkeley, CA: University of California Press.

Watson, Harry L. 1990: *Liberty and Power: The Politics of Jacksonian America.* New York: Noonday.

Chapter 16

The Southern Master Class: An Elite Woman's School Experience, 1838

Context

The South's planter elite was a small group. Half of the Old South's 385,000 slaveholders in 1860 owned one to five slaves but only 12 percent were planters, commonly defined as those owning 20 or more bondpeople. In 1860, three-quarters of white families owned no slaves. Despite their small size, the planter class exercised enormous political, economic, and cultural authority over their region. They were often the preeminent politicians, the economic brokers, and the cultural arbiters of their world. And they cherished their authority.

Dig a little deeper beyond the numbers, and we discover a class that was quite varied and textured, a class that had families, that possessed a set of values and harbored concerns that helped complicate the popular image of the master directing slave labor on his plantation. Yes, planters did manage their estates; yes, a few of them used overseers; and, certainly, many of them considered themselves Christian masters, ardent paternalists of their families, "black and white." But masters also considered themselves patriarchs of a sort, presiding over their households with almost as much authority as they liked to believe they had over their enslaved workers.

Southern planters were keenly interested in the raising of their own families and aimed to replicate the organic, authoritative form of social relations of their larger society within their households. Central to their view of the world was the role of southern women. The antebellum South – and much of antebellum America generally – was guided by the notion of separate spheres, the idea that men inhabited the public realm while women were custodians of the private household.

Antebellum women generally were charged with instilling moral values in children, for example. To some extent, this ideal had greater purchase in the North and was less prevalent in the South where plantation mistresses also managed labor and assisted in the running of plantation affairs, especially with regard to the management of slave labor.

The role of southern women was multivalent. Nearly all white southern women, especially elite ones, anticipated marriage and were expected to marry. Single women were often seen as too independent and contrary to masculine authority in what was, after all, a society that was very patriarchal. White women, however, sometimes encountered difficulties in meeting eligible men: plantations were spatially separated and the rural character of the Old South made it difficult to locate and foster eligible mates. Marrying a cousin or someone from the same county was not uncommon among southern white families since social interaction with extended family and neighbors was the norm. Cousin marriages made sense because they cemented family ties and business connections and helped consolidate land holdings. Historians have estimated that about one in ten marriages among elite antebellum North Carolina families took place between first and second cousins.

Courtship rituals varied a great deal and much of it was through letters. In such instances, the woman had to demonstrate penmanship and formal diction in an effort to reflect her pious, submissive, and proper behavior to her would-be husband. Southern women were also advised to curb their "passion." Many sought merely a "companionate marriage" – a soul mate for life but one that was sometimes emotionally distanced. Neither were women always free to choose their prospective husbands. Parents often played an important role in identifying and courting suitors and viewed their daughters' marriages with an eye to enhancing the status of the family.

While most southern women received no formal education in the antebellum period, the founding of female academies opened up new possibilities for elite white women, especially planters' daughters. After the Revolution, southern female academies sprung up in response to an emerging notion of "republican motherhood." The idea was guided by the belief that if the promise of the Revolution was to be fulfilled, then men would have to be virtuous and the role for preparing such men rested with women in the home. Women as prospective mothers therefore had to have some training. Sectional thinking was also at work here. Southern spokesmen considered that only educated mothers could counter the pernicious effects that slaves allegedly had on young children (especially since they grew up and played together). Others feared that northern abolitionist rhetoric could contaminate the minds of young southerners. Schooling and a mother's influence could temper these influences.

What, precisely, were women taught in these academies? Principally, the virtues of piety, submissiveness, and efficiency. Although female education was usually less demanding than males', by the eve of the Civil War the South had made significant advances in education. While the overall literacy rates in the South still lagged the North, the South educated men and women at roughly the same rate as in the North: in 1850, 16 percent of white women and 17 percent of white men in Mississippi attended school; by 1860 the respective proportions for men and women in Massachusetts was 22 percent of females and 23 percent of males. Elite southern women typically attended academies from two to four years, usually entering the academy between 12 and 14 years of age. Here, they met friends for life with whom they often maintained extraordinarily intimate and emotional bonds, bonds maintained through letter writing when they returned home.

Should she complete her schooling and should she meet and marry a member of the planter class, the white southern woman would join the small but influential ranks of the plantation mistress. Contrary to prevailing stereotypes, the plantation mistress, while obviously privileged in many respects, was required to work and work hard. Her principal tasks involved the management of household slave labor, which often proved frustrating and onerous, especially when slaves resisted in subtle and creative ways. On the whole, plantation mistresses had little in common with female slaves. Certainly, both were subject to patriarchal authority in the form of the master but beyond the commonality of gender, questions of race and class prevailed. In fact, plantation mistresses relied on the subordination of black women to give them leisure time and to define their own authority.

In the following letter, we catch a glimpse of a daughter of the white elite, a young woman who was in attendance at an academy in Columbia, South Carolina, in the late 1830s and who likely went on to become a plantation mistress (we cannot know for certain since details of Mary G. Davis's life are sparse). She recounts her experiences as a privileged white southerner at school, granting us access to the educational life of an elite young white woman of the Old South, the sort of subjects she was taught, the importance of establishing social ties with other elite white women, and the continued relevance of ties to her family.

Source

Mary G. Davis, Columbia [SC], April 14, 1838 to "Dear Sister" [Miss R. A. Davis], Darlington, [SC], South Caroliniana Library, University of South Carolina, Columbia, SC.

Columbia April 14th 1838

Dear Sister;

I received your letter, a month ago and have just commenced to answer it; I do not think I ought to answer it now, for I have heard of your laughing at me; so I expect you would rather I would not trouble you with my letters.
You asked me in your letter what progress I made in french, and music, I am in Mrs Martins second french class; as for music, Mr Martin does not give me any encouragement; though Miss Dufrey gives me enough but she only does it to get me to practice. I like Columbia very much, I think Mrs Martins an excellent school, though I do not think I would like it so much if it were not for Nathan.
I have seen Miss Tiny, and Miss Gracy Adams since I have been here Miss Tiny, inquired very particularly about you, and Miss gracy, about sister Harriet; Miss Tiny, sent her love to you, her sister asked me to go home with them, this week, but I could not go, I have been to but one dancing party, since I

[To the student: use this page to transcribe the text of the document on the opposite page]

have been in Columbia, and that was at Mrs Hamptons.
We are to have a May party. Sarah Scott is queen she is a very sweet girl. When will you return.
Do not let any one see this letter and do write to me. Give my love to sister Harriet, and Miss Lizy for me.

Your affectionate sister, M. S. Davis.

P.S. I received your last letter, Saturday evening, I believe I have answered every thing in it. We have a new boarder Miss Rowe, from Orangeburg. Do write to me, and tell me if you think I have improved any in letter writing.

[To the student: use this page to transcribe the text of the document on the opposite page]

Study Questions

1. Outline the nature of Mary Davis's formal education as suggested by her letter.
2. What seems to have been of greater importance to Mary Davis – formal schooling or sociability and intimacy?
3. Judging by the letter, suggest ways in which social networks were maintained and perpetuated among southern elites.

Further Reading

Bynum, Victoria E. 1990: *Unruly Women: The Politics of Social and Sexual Control in the Old South*. Chapel Hill, NC: University of North Carolina Press.

Clinton, Catherine 1982: *The Plantation Mistress: Woman's World in the Old South*. New York: Pantheon.

Fox-Genovese, Elizabeth 1988: *Within the Plantation Household: Black and White Women of the Old South*. Chapel Hill, NC: University of North Carolina Press.

Genovese, Eugene D. 1974: *Roll, Jordan, Roll: The World the Slaves Made*. New York: Pantheon.

Gutman, Herbert 1976: *The Black Family in Slavery and Freedom, 1750–1925*. New York: Pantheon.

Horton, James Oliver 1993: *Free People of Color: Inside the African-American Community*. Washington, DC: Smithsonian Institution Press.

Joyner, Charles 1984: *Down by the Riverside: A South Carolina Slave Community*. Champaign, IL: University of Illinois Press.

Kolchin, Peter 1993: *American Slavery, 1619–1877*. New York: Hill & Wang.

Levine, Lawrence 1977: *Black Culture and Black Consciousness: Afro-American Folk Thought from Slavery to Freedom*. New York: Oxford University Press.

McCurry, Stephanie 1995: *Masters of Small Worlds: Yeoman Households, Gender Relations, and the Political Culture of the Antebellum South Carolina Lowcountry*. New York: Oxford University Press.

McMillen, Sally G. 1990: *Motherhood in the. Old South: Pregnancy, Childbirth, and Infant Rearing*. Baton Rouge, LA: Louisiana State University Press.

Rawick, George P. 1972: *From Sundown to Sunup: The Making of a Black Community*. Westport, CT: Greenwood Press.

Stowe, Steven 1987: *Intimacy and Power in the Old South: Rituals in the Lives of the Planters*. Baltimore, MD: The Johns Hopkins University Press.

Chapter 17

Lives of the Enslaved: Urban Slavery in 1862

Context

In 1860, the South was home to just over eight million whites and just under four million enslaved African Americans. The vast majority of the enslaved lived and worked on plantations – large units of twenty of more bondpeople dedicated to the cultivation and export of profitable staple crops, principally cotton. Plantation labor was exacting. Slaves worked either in gangs – where their labor was directed by either a fellow slave driver, an overseer, or the master himself – or according to a task, a system used principally in the rice growing regions of the South in which slaves were assigned a daily task to complete and were then allowed to cultivate their own crops and tend to their own affairs. It was the labor of the enslaved, regardless of crop grown or labor system employed, that constituted the economic basis of the Old South.

As important as slavery was to the southern economy, slavery was also very much about the relationship between master and slave and how that relationship informed not only southern white perceptions of themselves and their society but how enslaved blacks managed to carve degrees of autonomy from a system designed to limit and circumscribe their freedom. After 1808, when the United States banned the importation of slaves, southern masters began to actively cultivate what some historians have described as a "paternalist" relationship with their slaves, a system, even way of life, that was at once kind but cruel, intimate yet manipulative, in an effort to encourage family formation among slaves and thereby make southern slavery self-reproducing and self-sustaining. Masters used a slanted version of Christianity and a variety of techniques not only to create sustainable, stable slave communities on their plantations but to fashion an image of themselves as benevolent, kind, and caring. Paternalism was a system that at once enabled masters to exercise great authority over slaves – the very formation of slave families, for example, allowed masters to use the threat of sale of family members as a way to enforce plantation discipline (indeed, between 1790 and 1860, roughly 835,000 slaves were sold, courtesy of an increasingly sophisticated internal trade slaving system) – while, at the same time, permitting slaves to carve out small degrees of autonomy within slavery.

In fact, southern slave society increasingly showed that while bondage was a very closed system, replete with mechanisms of control and exploitation, it was a system susceptible to imaginative resistance and manipulation. Slaves exploited paternalism – and in the very process, helped to define it – by appealing to the conceits of masters and mistresses, engaging in day-to-day resistance – such as feigning illness, turning privileges into customary "rights" and sometimes running away and even insurrecting. They also developed a meaningful, vibrant, and important slave community and culture, one distinct from that of whites and one largely outside of the purview of white society. Over time, antebellum southern slaves, especially on the larger plantations, created a slave culture that helped them weather the worst excesses of bondage. They resurrected African music and stories and reconstituted them in the context of southern slave society. Tales, stories, and fables in turn encouraged guile and mental agility, instructing young slaves in ways to fool masters and establish their own cultural lore. From music to hair styles, from clothes to food, southern slaves, while never obviously free from the constraints of bondage, nevertheless infused their world with their own social and cultural values, values that proved critical for the preservation and elaboration of their identity independent of southern planters.

Not all slaves worked on southern plantations. Although the slave South was far from being an urban society, there were towns and because they were in the service of the plantation South – serving principally as ports – they were important to the system. As such, they attracted both whites and slaves. Some whites, including plantation masters, lived in the South's major cities – such as Charleston, South Carolina, and New Orleans, Louisiana – on a seasonal basis, maintaining both a plantation and an urban dwelling. Other urban whites owned no or very few slaves. These tended to be skilled artisans, merchants, and other tradesmen who, although connected to the slave system, did not participate in plantation agriculture directly. By 1860, slaves comprised about half of Charleston's population and slaves were a significant presence in Richmond, Baltimore, New Orleans, and Savannah. They had been even more apparent earlier in the antebellum period and in 1820 in Charleston, for example, they actually outnumbered free whites and free blacks. According to some interpretations, urban slavery declined during the 1850s because slaves' ability to move with relative anonymity in urban environments was a distinct threat to social order. This worry, combined with an increase in cotton prices which led masters to relocate any urban slaves back to more profitable plantations, helps account for the gradual reduction in the number of urban slaves during the period.

Masters were often inclined to grant their urban slaves more latitude than they did those on plantations. Some would hire out their most skilled and trusted bondpeople to employers in southern cities both as a way to make money and also to reward slaves whom the master believed especially trustworthy. For their part, white employers of slaves negotiated with masters about terms of employment and because the system of slavery tended to deter the immigration of whites to the South, they frequently had little choice but to hire skilled slaves. Slaves who were hired out in this fashion undoubtedly enjoyed a degree of freedom denied their plantation brethren. Not only did towns offer greater opportunity for a little independence but they also afforded slaves a degree of geographic flexibility. While often subject to curfews and eyed by police, urban slaves developed small, often tightly knit communities and not infrequently used the cover of darkness to create and sustain friendships and generate their own income.

Here we have two related documents, both of which reveal the intricacies of urban slavery. The first details the hiring of planter John Dalton Warren's slave "Philip" to a baker in Charleston, Jacob Smalls. The second reveals a great deal about how Philip navigated his relationship with Smalls and Warren. It is possible that the letter is in Philip's actual hand and it is possible that he had learned to read and write while in Charleston (although we cannot know for sure – perhaps someone else wrote it on his behalf). Either way, Philip's voice, his wishes, are clear.

Sources

Document 1

Jacob Smalls to John Dalton Warren, Charleston, SC, November 5, 1862, John Dalton Warren Papers, South Caroliniana Library, University of South Carolina, Columbia, SC.

Document 2

"Philip" to John Dalton Warren, [Walterboro, SC], c. 1862, John Dalton Warren Papers, South Caroliniana Library, University of South Carolina, Columbia, SC.

Charleston Nov 5th 1862

I agree to take charge of Boy Phillip Servant belonging to Mr J. D. Warren of Colleton District, feed & cloth him while I am doing bufsines in the City.

Should it be nefsesary in my opinion to remove Servants. I wile send Phillip to Augusta or some Place of Safety if in my Power so to do, at the entire Expence of his owner Mr J. D. Warren, but I will in no way be responsible for said Boy should he run away or be captured by the Enemy. This permise is simply to show that said Boy Phillip is in my charge & will cease whenever notice is given to Mr Warren of my in ability to do so

Jacob Small

[To the student: use this page to transcribe the text of the document on the opposite page]

Dear Master

Dear Sir I am very sorry to inform you of this but duty bounds me to tell you that I have left Mr Smalley the reason why I will relate on last thursday evening one of his workmen forgot to make some particular bread for one of his customers I was serving the man at the time and after the bread wasnt made I thought it was no use to stay so therefore I did not the man came to him in the morning and ask him why did he not send the bread he then ask me why and I told him why and he then struck me in the face I then told him it was not my fault he took a tremendous large cowhide and cut me all about the face I wrote you this to tell you that I dont calculate to stay with him any longer I would willingly stay any wheres else and I wish you would come down and see him yourself before I go any wheres else I would have come to you my self but my face is so bad I would not go out any wheres when you are coming I wish you would write and let Mrs Keith know and I will go round there.

I Remains your
most humble servant
Philip

[To the student: use this page to transcribe the text of the document on the opposite page]

Study Questions

1. What were the terms of Philip's employment and what do they suggest about the relationship between the master class and skilled urban artisans in the Old South?
2. What is the nature and tone of Philip's complaint?
3. Do you think context might have been important in shaping Philip's decision? What was going on in the larger society when he left his employment?

Further Reading

Berlin, Ira and Phillip D. Morgan, eds. 1993: *Cultivation and Culture: Labor and the Shaping of Slave Life in the Americas*. Charlottesville, VA: University Press of Virginia.

Blassingame, John W. 1972: *The Slave Community: Plantation Life in the Antebellum South*. New York: Oxford University Press.

Curry, Leonard P. 1974: Urbanization and Urbanism in the Old South: A Comparative View. 40 *Journal of Southern History*, 43–60.

Genovese, Eugene D. 1874: *Roll, Jordan. Roll: The World the Slaves Made*. New York: Pantheon.

Goldfield, David R. 1991: Black Life in Old South Cities. In Edward D. C. Campbell, Jr. and Kym S. Rice, eds. *Before Freedom Came: African-American Life in the Antebellum South*. Charlottesville, VA: University Press of Virginia, 123–54.

Goldin, Claudia Dale 1976: *Urban Slavery in the American South 1820–1860: A Quantitative History.* Chicago: University of Chicago Press.

Levine, Lawrence W. 1977: *Black Culture and Black Consciousness: Afro-American Folk Thought from Slavery to Freedom*. New York: Oxford University Press.

Stevenson, Brenda E. 1996: *Life in Black and White: Family and Community in the Slave South*. New York: Oxford University Press.

Wade, Richard C. 1964: *Slavery in the Cities: The South, 1820–1860*. New York: Oxford University Press.

Chapter 18

The Modernizing North: A Businessman's Letter, 1836

Context

There is little doubt that the slave South, like the antebellum North, participated in the broader trend towards modernization in the antebellum period. Although the South did not urbanize or industrialize as quickly or to the same extent as the North, it did participate in commerce, it did participate in the market revolution, and southern agriculture did undergo a modernization of sorts, principally in terms of scientific agriculture and labor management. That much said, measured in conventional terms – industrialization, urbanization, and the growing use of wage labor – the North was a much more rapidly and thoroughgoing modernizing society.

The four decades following 1820 witnessed the fastest rate of urban growth in US history, much of it attributable to developments in the North. In 1820, for example, only 12 US cities had a population greater than 5,000; by 1850, there were nearly 150 such cities. Put another way, in 1820 about 9 percent of Americans lived in urban areas; by 1850, that figure was about 20 percent. In the same period, the Old South's south Atlantic population doubled but from a modest 5.5 percent to just 11.5 percent. In short, the North urbanized because it industrialized and attracted immigrants. The South did not industrialize to anywhere near the same extent and because slavery deterred immigrants from settling in the region, it remained overwhelmingly rural.

Industrialization followed a similar pattern. Before 1815, industry in virtually all areas of the United States was performed mainly in homes or urban shops by skilled artisans. Trained under an apprenticeship system, artisans owned their labor and oversaw the completion of a manufactured good from start to finish. There was little if any division of labor and artisans passed along their skills to other apprentices. In many northern homes, women were often the custodians of early manufacturing where they made finished articles from raw materials furnished to them by merchant capitalists.

After the War of 1812, this largely preindustrial, small-scale manufacturing system began to change, giving way to factories with machinery that could be tended by semi- and unskilled laborers and could produce finished manufactures on a larger scale at less cost. Again, the move toward an industrial society was predominantly northern. While most workers in the South remained tied to agriculture, northern workers increasingly became involved in industrial pursuits. The North had about two and a half times the amount of capital invested in manufacturing in 1810 as the South and three and a half times as much by the eve of the Civil War. The first northern factories were dedicated to the textile industry and were located mainly in New England, thanks to the availability of water power, emerging transportation networks, and the willingness of small groups of merchants to invest in industry. The first fully integrated textile factory was located in Waltham, Massachusetts, and the famous Lowell factory followed shortly in 1820.

Lowell in particular was supposed to be a model, distinct from and better than its English forebears. Lowell wanted to avoid the crime, poverty, and exploitation associated with factories in England and aimed to treat its workers in a paternal fashion, taking care of their spiritual and educational well-being, paying them well and generally creating an orderly and secure working and living environment. Above all, New England factories generally, at least those crafted along Lowell lines, aimed to instill in workers the values of sobriety, diligence, and thrift, values northern capitalists considered essential to their emerging industrial, modern order. Instead of relying on child labor, as many industrialists in England did, Lowell managers employed women, very often daughters of New England farm families. In the vanguard of America's industrial workers, these young women lived on site in boarding houses under the scrutiny of supervisors and they were encouraged to attend lectures and read. Discipline was strict and stiff fines were imposed for tardiness and talking.

As the factory system matured in the 1830s, the Lowell model was revised, especially in light of increasing competition among factories. Managers sought new ways to increase productivity and they upped workloads and cut wages. Worker resistance was met with dismissal, and factory owners, especially during the 1840s, began to hire cheaper, immigrant labor, notably the Irish who made up an increasingly larger share of the workforce in New England factories. Irish workers constituted a new and emerging proletariat. Unlike the Lowell women who tended to see their stint in factories as a temporary condition, Irish factory hands gradually became a permanent working class.

Class formation in the North was not simply about workers, however. An emerging middle class was also a product of northern modernization. This class included shopkeepers, professionals, and white collar workers. As manual and non-manual labor became increasingly distinctive, the northern middle class began to think of themselves in discrete terms and as a distinct social group. They enjoyed access to education and higher rates of upward social mobility than the working classes and, increasingly, lived in distinctly middle-class sections of towns and cities. They also held different values and embraced a particular aspect of evangelical Christianity, sentimentalism, and transcendentalism, all of which helped feed their burgeoning sense of individualism and self-reliance.

In short, a modernizing North shared those features of other modernizing, wage labor societies and came to resemble some European countries – particularly Great Britain – more than it did the slave labor South. Although a fully industrialized North would not develop until after the Civil War, the features were emerging in the antebellum period, features that increasingly made it different to the slaveholding, less urban, and less industrialized South.

The following excerpt from a letter written in 1836 articulates with places and people we have encountered in previous chapters. It was written by Joseph W. Patterson to Amos Lawrence – someone we have come across before (see Chapter 15) – and it refers to the National Road (see Chapter 13). Patterson seems to have been something of an acolyte of Lawrence's, trained by him in mercantile business in New England. Patterson writes to Lawrence from New Orleans about his travels westward and his impressions of economic and social development in America, apparently with an eye to establishing business links for Lawrence specifically, for New England generally. Patterson's eye is comparative and what he says reveals as much about his perception of northern society and its qualities as it does about his impressions of the newly settled mid-West and South.

Source

Joseph W. Patterson to Amos Lawrence, 21 December 1836, Amos Lawrence Papers, 1814–79, Box 2, Folder 11, Massachusetts Historical Society, Boston, Massachusetts.

At Wheeling we left the river and continued our journey by land over the National Road through Ohio — In the appearance of this State we were much dis-appointed — as, comparatively speaking, very little of it is cleared up — while we had supposed, from its large population, that the country would present a more social aspect. This State being in all parts very heavily timbered, has a less cultivated appearance than Indiana and Illinois with a much smaller number of inhabitants — the latter states having a very large proportion of prairie lands, easily subdued — Through all these states there is an air of comfort and competency — the houses have a fresh and tidy appearance and the tables are loaded with plentiful, though perhaps homely fare.

Cross the Ohio, and the scene changes — the contrast between the inhabitants seemed almost as great as between the English and French. For the first time, we now really felt ourselves away from New England, at least from some of the characteristics of its people — North of the Ohio is a population bent upon gain, industrious, sober minded and quiet — A people among whom one might feel every security for life and property — But not so upon the South — A lawless and quarrelsome spirit seems to pervade all classes — Among the higher orders you will hear of duelling and horse-racing — in a lower circle, you will hear and witness quarrelling stabbing and shooting — As little is thought of killing a person as of slaying an ox — And those who do not actually commit these deeds make up for the defect by loud talking and threats — Every person is well armed with sword-canes, bowie knives and pistols — One need not travel in a country to ascertain the character of its population, when he knows that such practices are allowed and followed — I think we have heard more profanity, and have seen more intoxication, in one week, since we have been in the Slave States, than we met with in the whole of our previous journeyings —

[To the student: use this page to transcribe the text of the document on the opposite page]

Study Questions

1. How does this letter compare to the documents offered in Chapters 13 and 15, especially with regard to economic development and sectional difference? What had changed by the mid 1830s, if anything?
2. What are the "social" qualities Patterson considers constitutive of New England and why might they be considered "modern"?
3. Why, in Patterson's opinion, was the South unlikely to share those northern qualities?
4. Was the mid-West beginning to resemble the South more than the North?

Further Reading

Bruegel, Martin 2002: *Farm, Shop, Landing: The Rise of a Market Society in the Hudson Valley, 1780–1860*. Durham, NC: Duke University Press.

Clark, Christopher 1990: *The Roots of Rural Capitalism: Western Massachusetts, 1780–1860*. Ithaca, NY: Cornell University Press.

Dawley, Alan 1976: *Class and Community: The Industrial Revolution in Lynn*. Cambridge, MA: Harvard University Press.

Dublin, Thomas 1994: *Transforming Women's Work: New England Lives in the Industrial Revolution*. Ithaca, NY: Cornell University Press.

Haltunnen, Karen 1982: *Confidence Men and Painted Women: A Study of Middle-Class Culture in America*. New Haven: Yale University Press.

Houndshell, David 1984: *From the American System to Mass Production, 1800–1932*. Baltimore, MD: The Johns Hopkins University Press.

Johnson, Paul 1978: *A Shopkeeper's Millennium: Society and Revivals in Rochester, New York, 1815–1837*. New York: Hill and Wang.

Prude, Jonathan 1983: *The Coming of Industrial Order: Town and Factory Life in Rural Massachusetts, 1810–1860*. New York: Cambridge University Press.

Ryan, Mary 1981: *The Making of the Middle Class: The Family in Oneida County, New York, 1790–1865*. Cambridge: Cambridge University Press.

Chapter 19

The Age of Reform: On the Need for Temperance, 1824

Context

The enormous changes wrought by the emergence of an expanded democracy, an industrial revolution, and urbanization, especially in the North, held both benefits and some significant social problems. Anxiety often accompanied change. In a nation where one could rise and fall quickly some people sought stability in religion while others attempted to check the excesses of a modernizing America by radically remaking institutions. The drive for renewal and order led to the emergence of a number of organizations and philosophies dedicated to reform, sometimes aiming to preserve old social institutions, sometimes to overturn them, sometimes to liberate, sometimes to control. This impetus was known as the Age of Reform and while it was a largely northern phenomenon, some aspects had purchase in the slave South.

Some of the impulse behind reform was born during the Second Great Awakening, which began in the early years of the nineteenth century and lasted well into the 1820s and 1830s. Initially centered on the frontier, the Great Awakening spread to towns, cities, and southern plantations. A good example of the braiding of reform and religion is apparent in the career of Charles Grandison Finney. In 1821, as a young man, Finney experienced a religious conversion that led him to give up his law practice and become an itinerant minister (he was eventually ordained in a Presbyterian church). Finney attracted national attention when he conducted a series of revivals in the 1820s and 1830s along the Erie Canal. Like George Whitefield before him, Finney had an entrancing voice and he used several techniques to inspire his listeners including protracted meetings, praying for sinners by name, encouraging women to testify in public, and placing those struggling with conversion on an "anxious bench" at the front of the congregation.

The Second Great Awakening, not unlike the First, was evangelical and stressed the need for individuals to undergo an emotionally wrenching conversion experience. Finney and other evangelical preachers rejected Calvinism and stressed instead free will and, by the 1830s, even argued for human perfectibility. Finney maintained that a true Christian should not rest until society at large was reformed and perfect. This message resonated with many people, but especially the northern middle classes. The market revolution and modernization had placed pressure on this class and although they viewed their success as a reflection of moral character they also feared losing their hard-gotten gains. Religion and the belief in progress and perfection offered them a way with which to cope with the fears, tensions, and uncertainties of their own lives.

The evangelical impulse had an added bonus from the middle-class perspective: The stress on progress and perfectionism also made for better workers and Finney's message was used by factory owners to stress the values of sobriety, frugality, and assiduity.

Finney's message also appealed to other northerners, workers and women especially. In fact, female converts outnumbered men by 3 to 2. Women, too, faced their own uncertainties – marriage was becoming less certain because of the migration of so many men westward – and many women joined churches, giving them a sense of community, purpose, and group identity. Churches also helped women become increasingly involved outside the home, especially in a variety of benevolent and reform organizations.

Not everyone sought comfort in religion. Some turned to other ways of thinking about the world. Romanticism emphasized the importance of emotion and intuition – not Reason – as the sources of truth. It applauded the unlimited potential of the individual who would soar if freed from the restraints of institutions, extolled humanitarianism and sympathy with the oppressed, and, for all of these reasons, reinforced the emotionalism of religious revivals, even though it tended to be most influential among American intellectuals. Like revivalism, Romanticism offered its own paths toward human perfectionism, most famously in the writings of Ralph Waldo Emerson who, like other transcendentalists, sought to rise above the material world. Romanticism, in short, helped intellectuals make sense of the changes in the market, economy, and polity occurring around them.

Revivalism and romanticism, with their emphasis on the desirability of improvement, progress, and perfection, gave rise to actual efforts to reform society. They took several forms, some aiming to reform American society from within, some by leaving it altogether. Some embraced Utopianism, hoping to reform society through withdrawal and example (such as the Mormons, the Shakers, and a number of collectivist, communal societies). Arguably, though, the most significant reform movements of the period sought not to withdraw from society but to change it directly. Such efforts varied enormously. Prison reform, for example, was popular. It aimed at not simply punishing people who broke laws but, rather, to treat them. Central to this idea was the building and design of new prisons, almost exclusively in the North, in an attempt to make criminals understand their crimes. The key to this understanding was the silent system, which regulated the sounds prisoners heard and could generate. The point of the penitentiary was to promote penance through silence.

There were other reform movements that attempted to redress problems in a variety of other areas – women's rights, education, treatment of the insane, among others – but two movements in particular drew widespread support and attention: the abolition of slavery and temperance. Abolitionism took many forms. One strain advocated moderate antislavery and called for colonization, gradual emancipation, often with compensation to slaveholders, and was headed by people who were not racial egalitarians. A more radical stripe of abolitionism was "immediatism." The immediatists were most closely associated with William Lloyd Garrison who called for immediate abolition and uncompensated emancipation. Garrison and his cohorts condemned slavery – and the South generally – as morally degenerate and their critique certainly contributed toward emerging sectional tension in the 1830s. Abolitionism generally was very much a product of evangelicalism and emotionalism but also a reflection of the emphasis on individual rights and the spirit of improvement and progress apparent in Romanticism.

For its part, southern society embraced few reform movements. An exception – and one that was genuinely national in scope – was the temperance movement. The origins of this reform movement against drinking lay in the era's high consumption of alcohol, which had soared after the Revolutionary War. By 1830 the per capita consumption was four gallons of alcohol a year, the highest level in US history and nearly three times today's level. Temperance advocates saw the consequences of drinking – broken families, abused and neglected wives and children, sickness, and crime – and attempted to combat it through secular and religious means. Clergymen were important to the movement and in 1826 the American Temperance Society was founded, making voluntary abstinence as its goal. In the next ten years about 5,000 local temperance societies were established and, by some lights, the movement was quite successful. By 1845, annual per capita consumption of alcohol had dropped to two gallons per year. The movement was perhaps more broadly based than other reform movements, attracting a wide variety of people including men and women of all classes, North and South. The accompanying document is a "Discourse for the Suppression of Intemperance," delivered on July 5, 1824, by the Revd Joseph Richardson of Hingham, Massachusetts and it captures precisely many of the reasons behind the formation of the temperance movement. Richardson was not only an ordained minister in the Unitarian Church in Hingham, he was also an active politician, serving as a Representative from Massachusetts in the US Congress and in the state Senate (he gave this speech while a member of the Senate). In other words, the links between religion, temperance, and political reform were often close and Richardson captures the broad social import of this aspect of the Age of Reform.

Source

Revd Joseph Richardson, an Independence Day "Discourse for the Suppression of Intemperance," delivered July 5, 1824, Ms. S-176, Massachusetts Historical Society, Boston, Massachusetts.

Our national blessings were purchased at a rate too dear ~~rate~~ to be passed by as mere themes for an anniversary celebration or as an occasion only of public festivity. The history of the world convinces us that civil liberty and religion spreads over man a friendly shade, not to indulge him in indolence and vicious repose, but to invigorate his moral powers and to cherish the virtues that add dignity to his character. It is by the insidious and enslaving power of vice that nations have been despoiled of their liberties. Every vice is an enemy to the prosperity of nations. Avarice subjugated the Greeks to the power of the Persians. What the Persian arms could not achieve was readily achieved by their silver and gold. When the Persians yield to the seduction of luxury and magnif[illegible] their glory declined.

[To the student: use this page to transcribe the text of the document on the opposite page]

The effects of this vice on the *mind* are no less deplorable. It reduces those faculties which God gave to constitute the chief ornament and dignity of our nature, in some cases to a state of idiocy. In a moment it strips the mind of all the graces of cultivation, of moral sentiment and refinement, and exhibits the mortifying spectacle of a monster in human shape. The tender affections, given to minister the sweetest solace in life, are turned into the madness and rage of the fell demon. In vain does conjugal tenderness appeal to the heart; in vain does filial respect implead the obligation of parental duty. Intemperance, the tyrant of tyrants, heeds not the plea. All reason and decency, all the holy sanctions of religion are set at defiance, till perhaps the midnight cry announces some tragic deed, that spreads horror through the peaceful village.

[To the student: use this page to transcribe the text of the document on the opposite page]

Study Questions

1. Identify what Richardson considers the chief effects of alcoholism.
2. Why does Richardson consider excessive alcohol consumption tyrannical?
3. Judging from this document, suggest reasons why the temperance movement had some impact not just in the North but in the South, too.
4. Can you detect other elements of the Age of Reform in the document?

Further Reading

Foster, Lawrence 1991: *Women, Family, and Utopia: Communal Experiments of the Shakers, the Oneida Community, and the Mormons*. Syracuse, NY: Syracuse University Press.

Ginsberg, Lori D. 1990: *Women and the Work of Benevolence: Morality, Politics and Class in Nineteenth-Century United States*. New Haven, CT: Yale University Press.

Hankins, Barry 2004: *The Second Great Awakening and the Transcendentalists*. Westport, CT: Greenwood Press.

Mayer, Henry 1999: *All on Fire: William Lloyd Garrison and the Abolition of Slavery*. New York: St. Martin's Press.

Petrulionis, Sandra H. 2006: *To Set This World Right: The Antislavery Movement in Thoreau's Concord*. Ithaca, NY: Cornell University Press.

Quist, John 1998: *Restless Visionaries: The Social Roots of Antebellum Reform in Alabama and Michigan*. Baton Rouge, LA: Louisiana State University Press.

Rorabaugh, W. J. 1979: *The Alcoholic Republic: An American Tradition*. New York: Oxford University Press.

Rothman, David 1971: *The Discovery of the Asylum: Social Order and Disorder in the New Republic*. Boston, MA: Little, Brown, and Company.

Schreiner, Samuel A. Jr. 2006: *The Concord Quartet: Alcott, Emerson, Hawthorne, Thoreau and the Friendship that Freed the American Mind*. New York: Wiley.

Stauffer, John 2002: *The Black Hearts of Men: Radical Abolitionists and the Transformation of Race*. Cambridge, MA: Harvard University Press.

Chapter 20

Westward Expansion: Kansas and Free Labor in 1856

Context

Given the emerging differences between a slaveholding South and a modernizing North, arguably the most pressing question on everyone's lips, certainly by the 1840s if not well before, was whether the West would resemble the slave South or the free North.

The urgency of this question grew over time and was not always indexed to the sectional question. Generally, Americans held a fascination with expansion through space in the antebellum period. There was a pressing sense of "Manifest Destiny," a term coined in the 1840s by John L. O'Sullivan, a Democratic newspaper man, who argued that it had become America's "manifest destiny to overspread the continent allotted by Providence for the free development of our yearly multiplying millions." Manifest Destiny embodied the sense that the US had a divine mission to extend democracy, freedom, and economic success westward, even around the globe. But in such an ideal resided darker elements and Manifest Destiny could be a handy justification for expansion and subjugating those in the way. For example, O'Sullivan went on to say about Mexicans: "they must amalgamate and be lost in the superior vigor of the Anglo-Saxon race ... or they must utterly perish." A similar mentality was also applied to Native Americans who, throughout the antebellum period, were pushed westward and forcibly relocated from their original lands.

Although Manifest Destiny was a credo embraced by northerners and southerners, underlying that shared value was a question that would become of enormous importance: whose version of freedom and the future would prevail in the West? At first, the two sides had managed to compromise as the country expanded, especially in the form of the Missouri Compromise of 1820. Recall that when Thomas Jefferson arranged for the Louisiana Purchase in 1803, the size of the United States increased tremendously. Almost immediately, Americans began to settle this territory. By 1819, several new states had been admitted to the Union creating a new balance of 22 states, 11 of which were free, 11 slave. The problem began in 1817 when Missouri petitioned for statehood. Slaveholders were determined that Missouri be admitted as a slave state, since they had already started to settle the territory, yet many northerners insisted that it be treated as a free state. After a great deal of debate, Congress struck a compromise that, for the time being, satisfied many in both sections. Missouri was admitted to the Union as a slave state while Maine, also petitioning for statehood at the same time, was admitted as a free state, thus preserving the ratio of free to slave states. More importantly, recall that by the terms of the Compromise, slavery was banned north of a line 36 degrees and 30 minutes and allowed south of that line. Although the Missouri Compromise is sometimes held up as an example of the two nascent sections' ability to fashion a compromise, even at this early date it suggests the importance of slavery in the evolving mindset of Americans and its special relevance when it came to westward expansion.

Sectional tensions mounted during the 1830s – witness the rise of abolitionism and the increasingly vocal defense of slavery in the South – and they did so in the context of rapid western settlement. From 1815 to 1850 the population of the region west of the Appalachians grew nearly three times as fast as the original thirteen states and a new state entered the Union on average every three years.

In 1836 Martin Van Buren, a New York Democrat, was elected President of the United States; in the same year, Sam Houston was elected President of the Republic of Texas. Mexico had agreed to Texan independence in 1836 after being defeated by slaveholding Texans but it was apparent to many that the Republic of Texas would become part of the United States. Should that happen, Texas, settled as it was by migrating slaveholders, would represent the addition of another slave state to the Union, a prospect that, from many northerners' perspectives, threatened to undo the delicate peace established by the Missouri Compromise.

From 1836 to 1845, when Texas was admitted to the Union, John Tyler and then James K. Polk machinated to admit the state knowing that the annexation would trigger a war with Mexico. Tensions between the two countries heightened and in May 1846 the United States formally declared war on Mexico after some minor skirmishes at Palo Alta and Resaca de la Palma. By September 1847 the Americans had captured Mexico City and occupied a substantial portion of northern Mexico as well as California and New Mexico.

Support for the war among Americans was mixed. Many slaveholding southerners fought for Texas because slavery was already well entrenched in the region. But northerners from both Whig and Democratic parties saw the war as a product of political maneuverings to expand slavery's influence in the West by something they termed "the Slave Power," a quiet, insidious group of slaveholders present in Congress. Some also argued that the presidency itself had been captured by southerners, who in turn had inspired the war in order to extend slavery, and they pointed out that Tyler and Polk were both southerners.

Sectional animosity over Texas and the War with Mexico (1846–8) increased with the introduction of a proviso attached to an appropriations bill (to pay for peace negotiations) in 1846 – the Wilmot Proviso. Initiated by David Wilmot, a Democratic congressman from Pennsylvania, the Proviso stipulated that slavery would be excluded from any territory acquired from Mexico as a result of the war. Wilmot was no abolitionist – he had fought vigorously against abolitionism and he had tended to support slavery in areas where it already existed – but he now argued, "the issue now presented is not whether slavery shall exist unmolested where it is now, but whether it shall be carried to new and distant regions, now free, where the footprint of a slave cannot be found." In part, Wilmot was being disingenuous since slaves were already in Texas. But he had identified what was to become the great issue of the next fifteen years: would slavery be allowed to extend to new regions as they became a part of the United States?

Even though Wilmot's proviso was rejected by the US Senate, it refused to fade from public discourse, instead acting as a symbol for northern antislavery forces seeking to check slavery's expansion. The Proviso also drew a wedge between southern Democrats who favored the expansion of slavery and northern ones (like Wilmot) who opposed it. Debate over the Proviso marked the beginning of the breakdown of the two-party system.

Why were southerners so concerned to expand slavery in the late 1840s? For several reasons. First, many slaveholders believed that unless slavery expanded it would die for want of productive cotton land. Second, many southern politicians argued that the Federal government had no constitutional right to prohibit slavery in new territories. They considered slaves property and maintained that the Constitution protected their right to take their property wherever they wanted. And third, many politicians in the South worried, quite properly, that, with faster population growth in the North, the only way they could retain national political influence was through territorial expansion. The stakes, then, were high, concerning not just labor systems, profitability, and morality, but political futures, too.

Americans, then, found themselves in a dilemma: their nation was important to them and, in good part, they framed that importance in the form of westward expansion. But inextricable to that issue was, increasingly, the question of slavery and freedom. That tension had been at best partially resolved – more realistically, simply postponed – in 1820. Now, in the late 1840s and early 1850s, it was threatening to unravel.

This excerpt of a letter, dated April 28, 1856, is from a Mr J. Newman, who appears to have been a supporter of the expansion of freedom – not slavery – in the West, specifically Kansas. His letter is to Nathaniel P. Banks, a well-known politician who was to become Governor of Massachusetts. Banks, at the time of the letter, had just been elected speaker of the US House of Representatives as a supporter of free soil and he was a keen observer of developments in the western territories. As we will see in the next chapter, a great deal was happening in Kansas in 1856 but Newman's letter is more concerned with what Kansas means broadly. This extract represents a clear statement on what the "West" meant to a supporter of free labor.

Source

Letter J. Newman[?] Kickapoo City, Kansas Territory, to Nathaniel P. Banks, Papers of Nathaniel Banks, Box 10, April 28, 1856, Manuscript Division, Library of Congress, Washington DC.

No answer

Kickapoo City Kansas Territory April 28th/58.

Friend Banks:

You will see from the date of this communication that I have at last reached my destination. I have been here some three weeks - and must say that I am highly pleased with the country. There are few places that present the same inducements to those who are desirous to procure for themselves not only a name and fame, but a fortune -. The emigration here is very large. We have a regular line of Packets, between this point and St Louis - very often see 2 and more Steamboats at our Wharf, at the same time. Besides the regular daily

[To the student: use this page to transcribe the text of the document on the opposite page]

line – there are a number of transient Boats. We have also a daily mail. Our place now numbers some 300 inhabitants – we have at the present time 64 buildings under contract. Kickapoo is 5 months old. Back of the town we have the finest country I ever saw; in fact I do not think there is a better country anywhere than the Salt Creek Valley of Kansas. We have a fine, deep soil, excellent springs and fine, never failing streams – plenty of timber for the present generation – an abundance of Coal – and a ready & free demand for produce. It is the country for farmers. Opportunities are daily presented, which a man having a small Capital could embrace

[To the student: use this page to transcribe the text of the document on the opposite page]

Study Questions

1. What were the attractions of Kansas for Newman?
2. Judging by his description, which system of social and economic arrangements seemed best suited to the state, slavery or free wage labor, and why?

Further Reading

Forbes, Robert Pierce 2007: *The Missouri Compromise and its Aftermath: Slavery and the Meaning of America.* Chapel Hill, NC: University of North Carolina Press.

Freehling, William W. 1990: *The Road to Disunion: I. Secessionists at Bay, 1776–1854.* New York: Oxford University Press.

Greenberg, Amy 2007: *Manifest Manhood and the Antebellum American Empire.* New York: Cambridge University Press.

Holt, Michael 2004: *The Fate of their Country: Politicians, Slavery Extension, and the Coming of the Civil War.* New York: Hill and Wang.

Johanssen, Robert W. 1989: *The Frontier, the Union, and Stephen A. Douglas.* Urbana, IL: University of Illinois Press.

Levine, Bruce 1992: *Half Slave and Half Free: The Roots of the Civil War.* New York: Hill and Wang.

Morrison, Michael A. 1997: *Slavery and the American West: The Eclipse of Manifest Destiny and the Coming of the Civil War.* Chapel Hill, NC: University of North Carolina Press.

Pletcher, David 1973: *The Diplomacy of Annexation: Texas, Oregon, and the Mexican War.* Columbia, MO: University of Missouri Press.

Potter, David 1976: *The Impending Crisis, 1848–1861.* New York: Harper and Row.

Stephanson, Anders 1995: *Manifest Destiny: American Expansionism and the Empire of Right.* New York: Hill and Wang.

Chapter 21

The Coming of the Civil War: Bleeding in Kansas, 1856

Context

One reason why the American Civil War did not erupt until 1861 – one reason, in other words, why the conflagration did not occur in the 1830s, 1840s, or 1850s – has to do, in part at least, with the existence of a two-party system that was national, not sectional, in scope.

The two-party system emerged in the 1830s and lasted until the early 1850s. It was comprised of the Democratic Party – the party of Jackson – and the Whig party. In general, Democrats tended to look to the past, believed in government intervention to protect the liberty of the individual, and were concerned about the rise of capitalism. Alternatively, the Whig Party looked to the future, feared excessive democracy, were generally procapitalist – they supported banks, touted the benefits of laissez-faire, and were ardent supporters of internal improvements – and were vocal nationalists. The key point to stress here is that it was not just the differences between Whig and Democrat that were critical, it was also their non-sectional nature. Both parties operated in the North and the South and this in turn ensured that disputes would be debated between parties and not between sections as long as the two parties remained politically viable.

Westward expansion and the concomitant emergence of the slavery issue placed enormous strain on this system. Following the Mexican War, for example, another question of territorial organization emerged: that of the admission of California to the Union. In 1850, Californians on the whole wanted to be admitted as a free state but, for reasons explained in the previous chapter, southern politicians objected, principally to preserve their claimed right to expand slavery in the future. As in 1820, the problem was resolved – at least superficially – courtesy of the continued, though ailing, functioning of the two-party system. The Compromise of 1850, as it was known, was really a list of five separate bills. The most important admitted California as a free state to the Union and, to pacify southerners, another bill provided for a more stringent Fugitive Slave Act which would facilitate efforts by slaveowners to reclaim slaves who had escaped to the free areas of the North. The Fugitive Slave Act was a point of real contention and served to further heighten passions with many northerners incensed that they were now obliged to help southern slaveholders reclaim slave "property." In truth, the Compromise of 1850 only deferred conflict. Moreover, it helped erode the stabilizing power of the two-party system. The Whig party was greatly weakened by the Compromise and there were significant splits on votes for the various clauses. Generally, northern Whigs voted against the

Compromise; southern ones for it. As a result, southern Whigs, even though many were proslavery, became increasingly associated with the northern wing of the antislavery Whig party. Increasingly, southern Whigs could not afford to be identified with the Whig party at all and the party died out by 1856.

By the 1850s, then, slavery as an issue, once swept under the carpet in the interest of national unity, moved to the forefront of national politics. The ideological and political climate created by the Compromise of 1850 allowed just three broad stances that politicians could offer voters when talking about slavery and its expansion. The Free Soil Doctrine, for example, maintained that it was the duty of Congress to prevent any further expansion of slavery in the West and insisted that no further concessions should be made to allow slavery in the territories. By the mid 1850s the Free Soil Doctrine had become the rallying cry of disaffected Whigs and some Democrats who were adamantly opposed to slavery. They would become absorbed by the Republican Party later in 1856. The southern counterpart to the free soilers was the States' Rights position which insisted, simply, that the federal government had no authority to rule on the question of slavery in the territories. Increasingly, this position became exclusively southern with extremely little support in the North.

The third alternative was the Doctrine of Popular Sovereignty. Here, the basic idea was that the question of slavery should be decided by those living in the territories. Championed principally by Senator Stephen Douglas of Illinois, popular sovereignty seemed like a viable answer to many, at least in the abstract, appealing, as it did, to basic tenets of democracy. But the idea had weaknesses. Most obviously, it assumed that people outside the territory would agree with the popular vote within the territory and that the vote would be an accurate reflection of the territory's views.

These problems became stunningly apparent in 1853–4 over the question of Kansas. By 1853 the territorial question had reemerged: what to do with the Kansas-Nebraska territory acquired as a result of the Mexican War? The answer was very much a test case for the Doctrine of Popular Sovereignty and the inhabitants of Kansas were left to decide their own future, known as the Kansas-Nebraska Act of 1854.

The Act revealed the limits of popular sovereignty from the outset. Proslavery southern forces and antislavery northern forces converged on Kansas in an effort to vote the territory into the union as a free or slave state with each group trying to rig the result through massive immigration. The two groups lived side by side, more often than not violently, and the battles and killings, which lasted until 1858, gave rise to the phrase "Bleeding Kansas." The result was messy and bloody and did a great deal to heighten sectional consciousness and animosity. Kansas was eventually admitted as a free state in 1861.

In the midst of the appalling violence in Kansas, an incident occurred in the US Senate that further excited sectional tensions. On May 19, 1856 Senator Charles Sumner of Massachusetts, a vehement and outspoken critic of slavery, delivered a speech entitled "The Crime against Kansas." It was an intelligent but vituperative speech and included a very personal attack on his fellow Senator from South Carolina, Andrew P. Butler. Sumner referred to Butler as "a Don Quixote" who "has chosen a mistress to whom he has made his vows, and who, though ugly to others is always lovely to him; though polluted in the sight of the world, is chaste in his sight ... [she is] the harlot slavery." Sumner's speech infuriated Butler's cousin, Representative Preston Brooks who, two days later, entered the Senate, approached Sumner and said: "I have read your speech with care and I feel it my duty to tell you that you have libeled my State and slandered a relative." Brooks then proceeded to beat Sumner senseless with the head of his cane. Sumner lay on the floor unconscious and bleeding profusely and it was over a year later before he returned to his Senate seat. Efforts to expel Brooks failed and he was subsequently fined just $300 and promptly reelected by South Carolinians.

The Kansas debacle and the caning of Sumner were a godsend for a new political force in the North: the Republican Party, a wholly sectional, northern party which drew its support from free soilers and former Whigs. Formed in the mid 1850s, it quickly grew in political strength and by 1858 it held control of the House of Representatives. The party's credo – free soil, free labor, free men – expressed its stance clearly.

And it was this party that ended up nominating Abraham Lincoln over Stephen Douglas for President in 1860. Although Lincoln made it clear that he did not intend to interfere with slavery where it existed, he did say he would stop its expansion and his election in November 1860 was understood by southerners as a direct attack on their peculiar institution, their political power, and their rights. Lincoln won by a purely sectional vote – he did not carry a single southern state – and many southerners began to consider it safer to exist outside the Union than remain in it.

If Kansas was so lush, as the previous document suggested, we might reasonably expect migrating southerners and northerners to be invested in the future of the state. As this document, from S. P. Hanscom suggests, they were. Five years before the outbreak of the Civil War, we can see glimmers of that great war in Kansas, a territory split by competing political interests. The territory was, indeed, a battleground. So-called "Border Ruffians" in support of slavery from Missouri established a powerful presence in Kansas, especially in Atchison, Kickapoo, and Leavenworth, and tried hard to influence elections through intimidation, violence, and ballot-stuffing. Northerners, such as Hanscom, responded in kind, arriving in Kansas in mid 1854 and establishing Lawrence, a free-soil settlement named after a figure we have encountered before, Amos Lawrence of Massachusetts. Free soilers established other towns such as Osawatomie in an effort to lend free soil weight to the territory. Violence was endemic and murders were not uncommon. Neither were armed raids, which exploded with force in the summer of 1856 when proslavery supporters burned Lawrence and when John Brown and free soilers attacked proslavery settlers at Pottawatomie Creek. Hanscom's letter reveals the nature of this struggle in grim detail. In some ways, the fighting in Kansas gave violent profile to sectional animosity and prefigured, albeit on a smaller scale, the terrible conflict that would erupt in 1861.

Source

S. P. Hanscom, Lawrance [*sic*] City, Kansas Territory, to Nathaniel Banks, April 26, 1856, Banks Papers, Box 10, Manuscript Division, Library of Congress, Washington, DC.

Lawrance City, Kansas Territory,
April 26 1856.

My Dear Sir:-

I enclose a list of the voters of Middleton in your District. It was forwarded to me at this place from Washington.

The Commission are holding sessions in this city. We have been to Lecompton the seat of Government, seen Gov Shannon who recieved the party courteously and extended evry facility to the Commission in his power. We made copies of the Roll Books and Census returns. The whole makes about 500 closely written pages of fool-scap.

An attempt has been made to drive the Commission from ~~at~~ this place by getting up arrests under the Bogus Laws. The shooting of Jones has been made the basis of a plea by Oliver and Whitfield that witnesses were afraid to come here, and Whitfield and his witnesses, on that account, left day before yesterday. The people of Lawrance, in public meeting have condemned the act of shooting Jones. The testimony so far is so strong against Missouri that Oliver is a good deal softened. We hope to get through by the middle of June. From here

[To the student: use this page to transcribe the text of the document on the opposite page]

the Commission will go to Leavenworth city where Gen. Whitfield is willing to appear with his witnesses.

Col Sumner arrived here night before last with 200 U.S. Dragoons from Fort Leavenworth under his command, having heard a report that the "Lawrence boys" had slaughtered his men detailed to aid Sheriff Jones, and he came to learn the fact himself. He was quite pleased to find that the contrary was the fact and that the people had so promptly condemned the assault upon Jones. He gave assurances that he would protect Lawrence with his troops should the Missourians undertake to attack the city. The excitement on the border consequent upon the attempt to kill Jones is great. He is recovering.

I Remain
Yours Truly
S. C. Hanscom

Hon N. P. Banks

[To the student: use this page to transcribe the text of the document on the opposite page]

Study Questions

1. What does Hanscom say about the nature of political corruption in the territory?
2. What forms of violence were of particular concern to Hanscom and why?
3. Did the fighting and tension erase all resemblance of democratic government and decency in Kansas?

Further Reading

Brock, William R. 1979: *Parties and Political Conscience: American Dilemmas, 1840–1850*. Millwood, NY: KTO Press.

Cooper, William J. 1978: *The South and the Politics of Slavery, 1828–1856*. Baton Rouge, LA: Louisiana State University Press.

Fehrenbacher, Donald 1981: *Slavery, Law, and Politics: The Dred Scott Case in Historical Perspective*. New York: Oxford University Press.

Foner, Eric 1970: *Free Soil, Free labor, Free Men: The Ideology of the Republican Party before the Civil War*. New York: Oxford University Press.

Hamilton, Holman 1964: *Prologue to Conflict: The Crisis and Compromise of 1850*. Lexington, KY: University of Kentucky Press.

Holt, Michael F. 1978: *The Political Crisis of the 1850s*. New York: Wiley.

Holt, Michael F. 1999: *The Rise and Fall of the American Whig Party: Jacksonian Politics and the Onset of the Civil War*. New York: Oxford University Press.

Nevins, Allan 1947: *Ordeal of the Union*. 2 vols. New York: Charles Scribner's Sons.

Potter, David M. 1976: *The Impending Crisis, 1848–1861*. New York: Harper and Row.

Rawley, James A. 1969: *Race and Politics: "Bleeding Kansas" and the Coming of the Civil War*. New York: J. B. Lippincott.

Silbey, Joel H. 1985: *The Partisan Imperative: The Dynamics of American Politics before the Civil War*. New York: Oxford University Press.

Chapter 22

Secession: A South Carolinian Describes the Event, 1860

Context

Lincoln's election victory in 1860 caused nothing short of a storm of protest, even hysteria in the South. Fear was the key. Southern politicians and the master class fretted that his election would spark off numerous slave uprisings, that Lincoln would abolish slavery, and that the South was now under northern political subjugation – that white southerners themselves were, in a sense, enslaved. These initial fears were so powerful and circulated with such rapidity that even ardent unionists in the South often became caught up in the general air of consternation. Talk of leaving the Union began to assume an unprecedented seriousness and gravity.

Republicans, however, tended to view such worries as typical of southern hysteria. After all, the South had threatened to secede before and Lincoln, at least initially, agreed with that assessment. Indeed, it is hard to see what the Republicans could have done to calm southern fears. In many respects the South's response was contingent not on Lincoln's election; rather, it was based on southern perceptions and anticipation of what Lincoln and the Republicans might do. As Lincoln said: "what is it I could say which would quiet such alarm?" "Is it," he pondered, "that no interference by the government with slaves or with the slave states is intended? I have said this so often already that a repetition of it is but mockery, bearing an appearance of weakness." Lincoln was also frightened of destroying his own party. To repeat his assurances might have alienated the antislavery wing of the Republican Party.

But the mood in the South only deepened and southern states began to meet in state conventions to consider secession. South Carolina acted first and on December 20, 1860, delegates to the secession convention voted 169–0 to enact an ordinance to dissolve "the union now subsisting between South Carolina and other states." Ardent South Carolina secessionists had hoped this would trigger a chain reaction among other, mainly lower south states. The New Year proved them right: Mississippi voted to secede on January 9, 1861; Florida followed a day later; then Alabama on January 11, Louisiana on January 26, followed by Texas on February 1.

Some southerners harbored serious reservations, however, and a minority desired some sort of cooperative action among individual southern states preceding secession to ensure a degree of unity. These "cooperationists" were, though, undercut by the swiftness of events. Another group of southerners, the "ultimatumists," urged a convention of southern states to draw up a list of demands to the incoming Lincoln administration. These demands included a more rigorous enforcement of the Fugitive Slave Act, guarantees against federal interference with slavery in Washington, DC, and against the internal slave trade, and an ironclad protection of slavery in the western territories. If the Republicans refused this ultimatum, then the South would secede. But the ultimatumists commanded little support in the state conventions mainly because many believed Lincoln and the Republicans generally would not agree to these terms.

For the most part, the movement to secede assumed an intensely emotional quality that rendered efforts to dilute it and engage rational discourse difficult. The movement was described by contemporaries as a storm, and it acted as a release of tension which had been building for years. It was a catharsis of sorts, a joyful act for many, one accompanied by festivities, dances, and social celebrations. In addition to its emotional, cathartic quality, secession was also perceived by many southerners as a dare they would win and thought it unlikely the federal government would resort to force to bring them back into the Union.

All efforts to compromise and resolve the crisis failed during the spring of 1861. Lincoln placed faith in the fact that the upper southern states had not seceded and that, of these states, most had elected unionists to their secession conventions. But Lincoln overstated the extent of Union sentiment in the Upper South. In fact, the Upper South was guided more by a notion of conditional unionism rather than unqualified unionism. These states would remain in the Union as long as there was no northern attempt to coerce the seceded states.

Time was not on Lincoln's side. Even as he was writing his inaugural address, some seceded southern states began seizing federal property within their borders, principally forts and arsenals. These events shaped Lincoln's speech and in it he stressed his determination to preserve an undivided union. He offered an olive branch and a sword: he promised not to threaten slavery where it existed but committed to using the power of the federal government to reclaim its property. Critically, he also told the South that "the government will not assail you, unless you first assail it." Lincoln was deliberately ambiguous as to how he proposed to protect federal property. Basically, Lincoln had hoped to buy time, but on the morning after his speech he found on his desk a dispatch from a Major Robert Anderson, commander of the Union garrison at Fort Sumter, South Carolina, stating that the garrison's supplies would last only a few more weeks.

Fort Sumter was a man-made granite island four miles from downtown Charleston at the entrance to the harbor. Even before seceding, South Carolina had expected the federal government to hand over Fort Sumter and the other nearby federal fort, Fort Moultrie. After seceding, state delegates went to Washington DC, to negotiate for the forts. Prior to Lincoln's inauguration, President James Buchanan had attempted to alleviate Fort Sumter's predicament by trying to resupply it by sending an unmanned merchant ship, the *Star of the West*, from New York. She was fired upon in Charleston, sustained minor damage, and turned back.

By the time of his inauguration on March 5, 1861, Lincoln was faced with a difficult situation. His options were limited. He could scrape together every available warship and soldier to shoot his way into the bay and resupply the fort but he was not sure if he could actually do it with the military forces he had available to him at the time. Moreover, should he follow this course of action, he would be blamed for starting a war and it might cause the Upper South to side with the Confederacy. Alternatively, Lincoln could prolong peace and keep the Upper South in the union by withdrawing the garrison and yielding Fort Sumter to South Carolina. But this tactic would divide the North, demoralize his party, perhaps wreck his administration, and acknowledge the Confederacy as legitimate, thereby sending the wrong signal to wavering foreign governments.

In the event, Lincoln elected to not attempt to forcibly resupply Fort Sumter. Instead, on April 6, 1861, he simply informed South Carolina Governor, Francis Pickens, that an attempt would be made to resupply the fort with provisions only and that, if the attempt met no resistance, the Federal government would make no aggressive move. The ball was now firmly in the Confederacy's court. President Jefferson Davis himself was increasingly under pressure to do "something" and he worried that popular support for the Confederacy was beginning to wilt under what was increasingly characterized as his "do-nothing" policy. As a result, on April 9, Davis, with the backing of his cabinet, ordered Confederate forces in Charleston to fire on Fort Sumter before the relief fleet arrived. The Confederates opened fire at 4:30 am on April 12 and 36 hours later Anderson was forced to surrender.

The war had started.

Excerpted here is a letter from Henry Campbell Davis of Ridgeway, Fairfield District, South Carolina, ("So Ca," as Davis writes it) written to his wife from the Secession Convention in Charleston. Davis was one of the signers of the Ordinance of Secession. This letter offers us insight into the mindset of the delegates and the atmosphere surrounding the decision of the first southern state to secede from the Union. It helps us understand how the secession process began, a process that ultimately led to the beginning of the Civil War half a year later.

Source

Henry Campbell Davis, St. Andrews Hall, [Charleston, SC], to "My Dear Wife," December 21, 1860, South Caroliniana Library, University of South Carolina, Columbia, SC.

St Andrews Hall
Dec 21st 1860

My dear Wife

I write to day from our Hall, while the Convention is in secret session. Yesterday the ordinance was passed which carried So Ca out of the Confederacy and she is now the sovereign and independent Commonwealth of So Ca. The ordinance was passed yesterday at 15 minutes past 1 O'Clock and last night at seven. it was signed by all of the Delegates. at Institute Hall, in the presence of the Gov. Senate and House of Representatives, and in the presence of about three thousand Citizens. It took two hours for all of the Delegates to sign it. Ladies were present, when it was signed and the President of the Convention proclaimed that So Ca was now a free and independent Commonwealth. The shout that went up from the persons in the Hall and the crowd in the street has never been equalled. All the night until late last night crackers, guns and rockets were [illegible] to in [illegible] the rejoicings

at the occasion. The act of passing the ordinance was a happy one to all of us. but I will write nothing more about it. as the papers are full of it

[To the student: use this page to transcribe the text of the document on the opposite page]

Study Questions

1. What, according to Davis's account, actually happened at South Carolina's secession convention?
2. What is the tone of Davis's letter?
3. Is it significant that he writes to his wife about this momentous political event?

Further Reading

Barney, William L. 1974: *The Secessionist Impulse: Alabama and Mississippi in 1860.* Princeton, NJ: Princeton University Press.

Channing, Steven 1970: *Crisis of Fear: Secession in South Carolina.* New York: Simon and Schuster.

Crofts, Daniel W. 1984: Secession Winter: William Henry Seward and the Decision for War. *65 New York History, 229–56.*

Crofts, Daniel W. 1989: *Reluctant Confederates: Upper South Unionists in the Secession Crisis.* Chapel Hill, NC: University of North Carolina Press.

Dew, Charles B. 2001: *Apostles of Disunion: Southern Secession Commissioners and the Causes of the Civil War.* Charlottesville, VA: University of Virginia Press.

Freehling, William W. 2007: *The Road to Disunion. Volume II: Secessionists Triumphant.* New York: Oxford University Press.

Snay, Mitchell: 1997: *Gospel of Disunion: Religion and Separatism in the Antebellum South.* Chapel Hill, NC: University of North Carolina Press.

Stampp, Kenneth M. 1950: *And the War Came: The North and the Secession Crisis, 1860–1861.* Baton Rouge, LA: Louisiana State University Press.

Chapter 23

Americans in Civil War: A Canadian Soldier's Experience, 1864

Context

At least initially, many Americans believed the Civil War would be a short affair. The Union thought it would be limited, a war simply to suppress an insurrection of seceded states, not one to physically destroy the South. For example, the Union General-in-Chief, Winfield Scott, simply planned to envelope the Confederacy and force it to reconstruct and return to the Union. This plan, known as the "anaconda plan," would take time, requiring an airtight naval blockade of southern ports and control of the Mississippi River. For many in the North, though, such a plan seemed timid and, increasingly, some newspapers urged Lincoln to attack the Confederacy at its heart in its new capital, Richmond, Virginia, and achieve a quick, offensive victory.

Jefferson Davis was also under pressure. Davis preferred a defensive war of attrition because he believed that the South could win by not losing. He aimed to hold fast, counter attack at Union weak points, wear out a better equipped foe, and compel the Union to give up by prolonging the War. But, like Lincoln, Davis found himself modifying his plan in the face of popular pressure. Confederate voices clamored to protect every part of the homeland and Davis had to scatter his forces thinly.

The Civil War was an immensely complicated event and there is little point in trying to list and examine every major military engagement. But it is worthwhile to point to certain accepted "turning points" during the War, not least because they suggest how the Union eventually came to prevail. And there were several such moments, on the homefront, on the field, at sea, and in the arena of diplomacy. For example, Britain's decision not to intervene on the side of the Confederacy was surely of great significance. Had Great Britain done so, the Union would have faced a Confederacy backed by the world's most preeminent nineteenth-century military power and the War might well have turned out differently. Then there was the Emancipation Proclamation of 1863, which Lincoln used mainly as a military tactic to weaken the Confederacy from within and which some historians see as injecting a moral purpose into the War.

Arguably, though, most historians of the Civil War have focused on key battles to suggest why the War turned out as it did. The battle at Antietam (or Sharpsburg), in Maryland, September 1862, is often considered a turning point in the War because of the weight that Confederate General Robert E. Lee placed on a successful invasion of the North. Lee aimed to invade Maryland, inspire a prosouthern uprising, then move northward. Lee hoped that Confederate success at Antietam might influence northern voters in the upcoming fall elections to declare themselves for peace and also bring about foreign intervention on the side of the Confederacy. As it turned out, Antietam was the bloodiest day of the Civil War and was understood, at least in the northern press, as a victory for Union General George B. McClellan. McClellan was praised for stopping Lee's invasion and Lee's failure to penetrate farther into Union territory convinced Britain not to step in on the side of the Confederacy and also gave Lincoln the opportunity to announce the Emancipation Proclamation.

Although some historians now stress the significance of Antietam to the outcome of the Civil War (it produced two major results), the battle at Gettysburg (July 1–3, 1863) still carries enormous scholarly weight and circulates powerfully in the popular imagination. And for good reason. Lee made a deeper penetration of the North at Gettysburg than at Antietam – in fact, Gettysburg was the northernmost major offensive launched by the Confederate army – and, as a military engagement, Gettysburg was the greatest battle of the Civil War. Nineteen percent of federals were either killed or wounded; the figure for the Confederates was a staggering 30 percent. More than sheer casualties, Gettysburg was also important because it sealed Britain's decision to abandon the prospect of intervening on the side of the Confederacy (Antietam merely led to Britain's postponement of the idea). The battle also deflated southern optimism more than Antietam and Lee was heavily criticized for the Confederate loss at Gettysburg.

With the fall of Vicksburg in May 1863 and William Tecumseh Sherman's subsequent gutting of the South's interior, especially in Georgia and South Carolina, the days of the Confederacy were numbered and their surrender in 1865 marked the close of America's costliest and bloodiest war.

What of the soldiers themselves during this appalling war? Why did they fight and what were their experiences? These questions have begun to occupy historians' interest in recent years and their findings suggest that Confederate and Union soldiers fought often for similar reasons. Many Confederate soldiers, for example, saw the Civil War as a second war for independence, a war to save them from what they perceived as northern tyrannical rule. Many Union troops felt similarly, although from a different vantage point. Union troops too thought they were fighting to uphold the legacy of 1776 and fought against the anarchy of secession, for the freedom of future generations, and against the threat that the Confederacy posed to American nationalism and republican liberty. There were, to be sure, important differences. Confederates were especially sensitive to the idea of defending their homeland from an external invader and very concerned with the preservation of southern values, including the defense of southern womanhood. Union forces did not share such concerns. In fact, because roughly a quarter of Union troops were foreign-born, they tended to draw direct comparisons with their largely European experience and defense of liberty against aggressive foes (such, especially, was the case with Irish-born Union soldiers).

The excerpt offered here speaks to the questions of who fought in the War, their daily experiences, and suggests the international dimension of the American Civil War. The letter was written by Francis Wafer, of Kingston, Canada West, who was an assistant surgeon with the 108th New York Infantry. Wafer fought for reasons similar to those motivating northern-born, Union soldiers. Some Canadian – and foreigners generally – fought because they had no choice. Some were kidnapped and forced to serve; others happily fought for money; still others because they believed in republican ideology and liberty, a conviction that tended to make Canadian soldiers more attuned to the Union than to the Confederacy. Canadians enlisted in over 250 Union regiments and 50 Confederate ones and participated in every major battle and many minor skirmishes.

Numbers are spongy generally and ascertaining how many Canadians fought for the Confederacy has proven tricky. The numbers estimated to have served in Union regiments range from between 15,000 to 100,000. But these figures are probably unreliable too. Because Canada was, at this time, still part of the British Empire and because enlisting in a foreign army was against British law, many Canadians who did join Union or Confederate regiments did so anonymously and lied about their place of birth. The term "Canadian" itself is also problematic. Canada did not begin to achieve independence from Britain until 1867, two years after the end of the War, and while it might be accurate to talk of an incipient Canadian nationalism in the early 1860s, it is, technically, misleading to talk about a Canadian state that had not yet come into existence.

This particular letter says little about motivation but more about the experience of war. It was written toward the end of the War. Wafer notes the "new lieut general U S Grant" and his command of the Army of the Potomac – a reference to Grant's promotion to the grade of Lieutenant General in late 1863 (a rank last held by George Washington) when he was given command of all Union armies. Wafer likely wrote this letter from Morton's Ford in Virginia in March 1864, where, a month earlier (February 6–7), the 108th New York Volunteers had been involved in an inconclusive engagement with Confederate forces led by Richard S. Ewell. The importance of this letter resides in its description of daily life, the experience of soldiering, and soldiers' awareness of the larger course of the War.

Source

Francis Wafer to "Dear Brother," Hd Qur 108th New York Vols, Martins Ford [Morton's Ford?], Va., March 20, 1864, entry in "2 Years in the Army of the Potomac: Events of the Campaign in Virginia, the Diary of a Surgeon, 1861–1863," Queen's University Archives, Kingston, Ontario, Canada.

Yours of the 18th past received in this even
ings mail was beginning to feel the time of your response long
But better late than not at all. Did you realize the value a
soldier sets upon the meanest letter, you would be more prompt
in writing. Health excellent, indeed I believe you would not
know me, since I made my escape from your —— climate
living in houses & sleeping upon those —— feather beds, enough
to kill any soldier. Without joking I was a candidate for
sick leave, when I returned to camp. No wonder after what
I had just passed through. First came the battle of the 6th Feb.
where in searching for our wounded at night I became heated
then laid down in our line to rest with the bridle on my
arm, fell asleep & got chilled. Next four days operating &
dressing in field hospital. Then a long journey & the only treat
ment for my cold to apply more cold, & that of the Canadian
kind. Then another journey, not taking into account the em
otion & excitement. I think I escaped well, when I complain
ed of nothing worse than "railroad on the brain." All has been
quiet since my arrival, except some trifling alarms ow
ing to some increased activity among the enemys pickets,
we have packed up twice. We expect "something to be did"
now. The new Lieut General U S Grant it is said will
remain with the Army of the Potomac in the coming cam
paign. Have passed my time since pretty agreeably under
the circumstances. The camp has been quite lively owing
to the presence of so many ladies who have just been order
ed home for fear of a movement. The weather is lovely, & the
splendid bands of the Brigade make the whole surrounding
air warble with their music, at guard mounting at 8 in
the morning & dress parade at sunset, besides their fre
quent serenades of ladies & popular officers fine evenings

[To the student: use this page to transcribe the text of the document on the opposite page]

Study Questions

1. Does the letter give any hint of Wafer's political views or suggest why he fought for the Union?
2. What was daily life like for Wafer? What bothered him the most and what were his sources of joy?
3. What sort of news about the War reached Wafer?
4. What does this letter suggest about the nature of nationalism in the mid nineteenth century?

Further Reading

Berlin, Ira et al. 1992: *Slaves No More: Three Essays on Emancipation and the Civil War.* New York: Cambridge University Press.

Cashin, Joan, ed. 2002: *The War Was You and Me: Civilians in the American Civil War.* Princeton, NJ: Princeton University Press.

Cougle, Jim 1994: *Canadian Blood, American Soil: The Story of Canadian Contribution to the American Civil War.* Toronto: Civil War Heritage Society Press of Canada.

Faust, Drew Gilpin 1988: *Confederate Nationalism: Identity and Ideology in the Civil War South.* Baton Rouge, LA: Louisiana State University Press.

Faust, Drew Gilpin 1996: *Mothers of Invention: Women of the Slaveholding South in the American Civil War.* Chapel Hill, NC: University of North Carolina Press.

Lonn, Ella 1951: *Foreigners in the Union Army and Navy.* Baton Rouge, LA: Louisiana State University Press.

McPherson, James 1997: *For Cause and Comrades: Why Men Fought in the Civil War.* New York: Oxford University Press.

McPherson, James and William J. Cooper, Jr., eds. 1998: *Writing the Civil War: The Quest to Understand.* Columbia, SC: University of South Carolina Press.

Mitchell, Reid 1988: *Civil War Soldiers.* New York: Viking.

Rawley, James A. 1989: *Turning Points of the American Civil War.* Lincoln, NE: University of Nebraska Press.

Chapter 24

Emancipation: The Labor of Freedom, 1867

Context

What did it mean to be "free" for the four million or so southern bondpeople emancipated by the Civil War? What tactics did southern planters use after the War to try to reinstate their authority, to place strictures on the people they had once owned as slaves but were now their "employees"?

In truth, there was no one definition of freedom at work in the Civil War and postbellum South. Moreover, freedom did not come all at once. Often, it was contingent on the proximity of the Union army. Some African-American slaves experienced a degree of freedom as early as 1861 because many ran to Union lines where they became contraband. Others were kept in ignorance of the 1863 Emancipation Proclamation (which freed very few slaves anyway) and the Thirteenth Amendment (1865) by their masters, sometimes for a year or more after the War had ended. On the whole, though, most southern slaves learned about their freedom between 1863 and 1865.

Just as timing varied, so did reactions. Some slaves were told by their maters that they were no longer enslaved and, upon hearing the news, many celebrated. Others were simply shocked, unable, initially at least, to process the information, to comprehend the news they had just heard. Still others were initially suspicious and thought that what they had been told was a way to test their fidelity. Some newly freed slaves viewed freedom with fear. They did not – could not – know what freedom would hold.

Many southern whites assumed that blacks encountered freedom in total ignorance. They were wrong. Freedpeople had definite, if diverse, ideas about what freedom meant and how they wanted to exercise it. Many ex-slaves defined freedom in simple contradistinction to slavery. Under slavery, for example, slaves were often forced to go by a number of names, such as "boy" or to take their master's last name. Many had no last name at all. But with freedom ex-slaves took new names defined by themselves, symbolically overthrowing their erstwhile master's authority. Some took the names of former presidents, others names that reflected their aspirations about what freedom would bring: Deliverance Berlin, Hope Mitchell, Chance Great. Taking "Freedman" as a last name was not uncommon. Ex-slaves also defined their freedom by rejecting old habits of white surveillance. Under slavery whites had restricted the ability of slaves to move about, meet, and gather. Freedpeople now held mass meetings and conducted their own religious services. No longer required to carry a pass, freedpeople also exercised their freedom by simply traveling, sometimes great distances. Increasingly, freedpeople moved to urban areas where they could find jobs and begin to establish new lives.

Of all the motivations for black mobility, none was more poignant than the effort to reunite families separated during slavery. For many freedpeople, freedom was incomplete until they were reunited with loved ones and many advertised in newspapers to relocate sold kin. Typical of such advertisements is the following, from the Nashville *Colored Tennessean*, in 1865: "during the year 1849 Thomas Sample carried away from this city, as his slaves, our daughter, Polly and son ... we will give $100 each for them to any person who will assist them ... to get to Nashville, or get word to us of their whereabouts." Sadly, such efforts often ended in failure or, in cases where spouses had remarried, profound disappointment. But freedom did allow ex-slaves to reaffirm their current family and many legalized their marriages immediately following emancipation.

Religion was also critical for defining freedom. For most of slavery, the religion of slaves was prescribed by masters who frequently extolled the putative virtue of obedience. Slaves were rarely allowed to attend church and when they did they were required to worship in biracial congregations, under the purview of whites.

In short, slaves' religious life (at least formally) was intended to be under the control of white masters. Emancipation changed this. What had previously been an invisible institution of black religion practiced in the secrecy of slave cabins now emerged and freedom witnessed the wholesale withdrawal of blacks from biracial churches. Blacks pooled their resources, bought land, and established their own churches. The shift was dramatic. In 1860, 42,000 black Methodists worshiped in biracial South Carolina churches; by the 1870s only 600 remained. Instead, many ex-slaves joined the African Methodist Episcopal church which became one of the biggest black religious organizations in the South.

Perhaps the most striking illustration of freedpeople's quest for self-determination was their seemingly unquenchable thirst for education. Before the War most southern states prohibited the instruction of slaves and the majority of slaves were, therefore, illiterate. After the War, freedpeople went to great lengths to learn how to read and write and took full advantage of northern missionaries and the Freedmen's Bureau, both of which identified education as critical to the fulfillment of freedom. Ex-slaves wanted to learn how to read and write so that they might better understand the Bible and the provisions of labor contracts offered them by southern planters immediately after the War.

Ex-slaves also came to define their freedom by inheriting the values of white American society, especially northern values concerning the "responsibilities" of freedom. In other words, freedpeople could not conceive of freedom merely in relation to slavery and many ended up defining it, additionally, in accordance with the values of white, bourgeois society. And, in the reality of a post-emancipation society, ideas about work, the relationship between wage and labor power, notions of contract and legal obligation, as well as philosophies regarding work ethic and discipline came to play an important role in the way that ex-slaves understood the responsibilities as well as the rights of freedom. Although freedpeople defined slavery as the freedom to labor for themselves, they were bombarded with definitions of what responsible labor meant, not just from southerners but from northerners too, especially the Freedmen's Bureau whose officers argued that real labor was the right to sell one's labor for a wage. To earn a wage, they were told, you had to work hard and diligently, had to be punctual and assiduous. Much of this proved unpalatable to many freed slaves because free wage labor, measured by the hour, was, in their eyes, little more than a different form of slavery. Instead, what freedpeople wanted was independence, not necessarily the right to sell their labor but, rather, to use their labor for themselves by producing goods on their own farms and for their own consumption. But because planters still owned most of the land in the postbellum South, many freedpeople found themselves coerced into working for former masters on terms that seemed little different to slavery.

The document presented here – entries from a plantation journal from South Carolina kept in 1867 by a former master – reveals with wonderful precision not only the ways in which postbellum planters attempted to control and discipline black labor but also how freedpeople attempted to exercise their freedom. John Forsythe Talbert, like many planters immediately after the War, attempted to discipline the labor of freedpeople by both deducting wages for time lost and by extending credit – and, therefore, control – to freedpeople for miscellaneous items. Ostensibly, the entries say a great deal about labor relations in the New South; they also say a great deal about the choices ex-slaves made in trying to define their freedom.

Source

John Forsythe Talbert Plantation Journals, Edgefield District, SC, vol. 4, South Caroliniana Library, University of South Carolina, Columbia, SC.

Chisly – Freedman – Dr.

To Jno. F. Tallent

1867

January	10th	To four dollars in cash – advance on wages in Augusta	$4.00
~~Jan~~	~~[illegible]~~	To $2.00 for pair Shoes for Susan	2.00
	30th "	" 1 Overcoat	3.00
Feby.	1st	" ½ gal. Molasses	.50
"	9th	" 1 pair Shoes from W. G. 2.	3.50
"	12th	" 1 quart Molasses	.25
"	15th	" 1 do. do.	.25
	23rd	" 1 quart do	.25
	30th	" Two dollars (order on Parks	2.00
April	4th	To 1 pair Shoes	2.25
"	[illegible]	To 2 dollars cash in Augusta	2.00
May	11th	" 30 cts – worth Sugar	.30
June	7th	" 1 [illegible]	1.00
"	9th	" 3 lbs Bacon @ 20cts.	.60
"	"	" 1 lb. Sugar	.20
"	13th	" 1 Hat – [illegible]	2.00
	29th	To Order for 5 dollars for [illegible]	5.00
[illegible]	[illegible]	To 80 cts for The Bucket	.80
August	17th	To 5 dollars advanced [illegible]	5.00
[illegible]	12	" One [illegible] flour	1.00
"	18	" 1 quart Molasses	.20
Oct.	12th	" ½ Gal – Syrup	.40
"	21st	To post-pay for Mullens for [illegible]	.33
Nov.	9th	To Order on J. J. Shippen	4.00
Decr.	7th	To 3 yds. Osnaburgs	.60
	16th	" 5 dollars advanced in Augusta	5.00
	22nd	" [illegible] (20 cts) [illegible]	.20
	24th	Cash advanced 2 dollars, also 5 dolls	$46.63
			7.00
			53.63

[To the student: use this page to transcribe the text of the document on the opposite page]

1.

Account of lost Time of [illegible] & wife Susan for the year 1868

			day	hr	minutes
April	29th	– Lost in getting to work	0	–	15
May	26th	= Lost from dog Bite	1/2	"	"
	27th	" " " "	1	"	"
	28th		1	"	"
	29th	" " " "	1	"	"
	[illegible]th		1		
July	23th	[illegible] to [illegible] –	"	"	30
Novr	19th	– Lost in going to election –	1	6 "	"
"	18th	– Lost in coming home from the election	0	" 2	" 0

[To the student: use this page to transcribe the text of the document on the opposite page]

Study Questions

1. What sort of items did the freedman in Talbert's account "buy"? What was his level of indebtedness by the end of 1867?
2. How might that indebtedness have been used by Talbert?
3. What does the document suggest about the ways in which freedpeople chose to exercise their freedom – and the costs involved in those choices?

Further Reading

Edwards, Laura F. 1997: *Gendered Strife and Confusion: The Political Culture of Reconstruction*. Urbana, IL: University of Illinois Press.

Foner, Eric 1984: *Nothing but Freedom: Emancipation and Its Legacy*. Baton Rouge, LA: Louisiana State University Press.

Glymph, Thavolia and John Kushma, eds. 1985: *Essays on the Post-Bellum Southern Economy*. College Station, TX: Texas A&M University Press.

Hahn, Steven 1990: Class and State in Postemancipation Societies: Southern Planters in Comparative Perspective. 95 *American Historical Review*, 75–98.

Roark, James L. 1997: *Masters without Slaves: Southern Planters in the Civil War and Reconstruction*. New York: Oxford University Press.

Saville, Julie 1995: *The Work of Reconstruction: From Slave to Wage Laborer in South Carolina, 1860–1870*. New York: Cambridge University Press.

Silber, Nina 1993: *The Romance of Reunion: Northerners and the South, 1865–1900*. Chapel Hill, NC: University of North Carolina Press.

Stanley, Amy Dru 1998: *From Bondage to Contract: Wage Labor, Marriage, and the Market in the Age of Slave Emancipation*. New York: Cambridge University Press.

Tunnell, Ted 1984: *Crucible of Reconstruction: War, Radicalism, and Race in Louisiana, 1862–1877*. Baton Rouge, LA: Louisiana State University Press.

Zuczek, Richard 1996: *State of Rebellion: Reconstruction in South Carolina*. Columbia, SC: University of South Carolina Press.